OPERATION CROSSROADS AFRICA

Operation Crossroads Africa

by RUTH T. PLIMPTON

THE VIKING PRESS

New York

To Cal,
David, Tommy, Polly, and Teddy

Acknowledgments

James H. Robinson should have written this book, but he was too busy "living" the events. Hence it became my privilege to write about Crossroads, and with the support of Reverend and Mrs. Robinson every inch of the way, it was a real pleasure.

Many courtesies were shown me by the Crossroads staff, both in New York and in Africa. The task of moving from one work project to another was greatly enlivened by Leo Sam, John Hubbell, John Williams, and Ronald Davidson.

I am deeply grateful to all Crossroaders for the honest and generous way they have communicated their adventures and emotions. The text has been considerably enriched by the writings of Adele Smith, Cathy Cobb, Tommy Holihan, and Andrea Cousins. I am equally grateful for the many other thoughtful letters. Every letter, journal, and conversation shared has somehow influenced the writing of this book.

Studying Crossroads proved to be the gayest form of research. Each group received me with such genuine warmth that, although I always felt like a visitor upon arrival, I was a member by departure. My thank-you notes are addressed to their leaders: Perry M. Sturges in the Republic of the Congo, Hugh and Beth Nelson in Northern Rhodesia, Tilman C. Cothran in Kenya, Nola Jean Hatten in Nigeria, Vernon L. Ferwerda in Dahomey, Mia Choumenkovitch in Togo, Antonio Blackburn in Ghana, Gerard Mertens in Ivory Coast, Clarence D. Jayne in Liberia, Minoru Mochizuku in Sierra Leone, Willard R. Johnson in Guinea, and Naomi M. Garrett in Senegal.

I shall never forget the African hospitality. The Africans outdid themselves equally in the smallest mud huts and in the most luxurious homes. These hosts were too numerous to list. I can only hope that some of them may experience American hospitality, and that it will come somewhere near their standard.

vii

Besides the Crossroads writers already mentioned, there are several Crossroaders who have given me special help on particular chapters: Mia Choumenkovitch and Tom Gilhool on Togo; Trevor Garwood-Jones and Bill Freeman on Ghana; Peter Bell on the Ivory Coast; Jane Martin and Mary Frances Reed on Liberia; Willard Johnson and Bill Davis on Guinea; and Betty Ann Rabb on Mali and Senegal. They have been intellectual stimulants as well as sources of information.

To the following people I owe thanks for reading the entire manuscript with very helpful criticism: James H. Robinson, Gwendolen M. Carter, Richard P. Unsworth, Lindsay H. White, and my best critic and constant encourager, Calvin H. Plimpton.

Half of the pictures on the end covers were taken by Thecla Haldane, a professional photographer. She is most generous in letting me use them.

Last but not least, it was our son, David Plimpton, who introduced me to Crossroads, and Jean Swartzbaugh who had the wit to suggest, "If you're so interested in Crossroads, why don't you write a book about it?"

Many student groups besides Crossroads have become recently active in Africa. It is not out of lack of respect that I have failed to mention them. Writing about Crossroads is like writing a biography. One concentrates on the chosen subject matter and leaves it to the reader to make comparisons with other familiar characters.

Contents

Preface

by

Adlai E. Stevenson

OUR AGENDA OF PUBLIC AFFAIRS IS A LONG ONE THESE DAYS, PILED high with items on which it behooves us to do our homework. Nor is it easy to assign priorities and say this is more urgent than that. The plain fact is that a citizen's duty today requires devoted attention to many problems, on whose solution depends not only our continued peace and prosperity but perhaps our continued existence as a free people.

Among these problems, one of the most urgent is to find means of establishing decent human relations between the white majority of the United States and the colored majority of the world. Our success or failure here will depend, in the first instance, on what we do or fail to do in the area of race relations at home. Continued discrimination and segregation in New Orleans—or in New York—will undermine our best efforts abroad. We are making pretty good progress at home. We must try to make good progress abroad. And the testing place is Africa.

This book describes one of the key experiments now being conducted to establish a decent human relationship between Americans and Africans. It is not an easy task. Mrs. Plimpton says at one point: "The Crossroaders were in a position to inherit

some of the bitter and suspicious attitudes stimulated by the relationships of the past." This sentence happens to describe a Crossroads work group in a former French colony. It could equally well
describe reactions throughout Africa, where the emotional fallout
of colonialism affects gravely the average African attitude toward
Americans, no matter how friendly their motives.

Like the Peace Corps, Operation Crossroads Africa has dem-
onstrated, by deeds not words, the friendly feelings of Americans
—and Canadians, to be sure—toward the citizens of the newly
independent states of Africa. This demonstration takes the form
of practical manual labor on projects of value to the local community—schools, hostels, drainage ditches, and the like. The work
is done by young men and women of all races, creeds, and colors,
who labor side by side with their African student counterparts.
But the projects, useful as they are intrinsically, are not as significant as the intangible by-products of the experience itself:
heightened awareness, deepened understanding, renewed demonstration of the dignity of manual labor; above all, practical evi-
dence that the affluent North American society *cares* about African
society.

For those who fret about American youth today the book
must be enormously reassuring, if only for its revelation that many
times more young people apply for Crossroads each year than can
be accepted; and they pay a large part of their own way, to go
and labor in the sun! Not only that, but all those who go must
agree to make at least one speech a week to local clubs and organizations about their experiences for a year after they return home.
The result of this must be a greatly increased awareness of Africa
in community groups across the nations.

Mrs. Plimpton, in telling the human story of Operation Crossroads Africa, makes it clear how this organization, entirely private
and voluntary, without government sponsorship or support, nevertheless is directly relevant to our foreign-policy aims. To paraphrase
Clemenceau, one might say that, today, foreign policy is too important to be left to the governments. Citizens must involve them-

selves in meaningful relations with citizens of other countries. Crossroads is a shining example of a people-to-people relationship that works.

But I would not wish to leave the impression that this is a sober tome on foreign policy. It is a lively, fresh, candid account of a variety of individual human experiences and reactions, with the frustrations and difficulties, as well as the achievements and joys, that go with any good human work. It is also an introduction to a wide American audience of that remarkable American whose lengthened shadow *is* Crossroads: the Reverend James H. Robinson, named after the kindest of the three masters for whom his grandfather was a slave, who grew up out of the Knoxville "Bottoms" to become a Presbyterian minister, founder of the Church of the Master in Harlem, then founder and now full-time director of Operation Crossroads. All of us, I think, can be proud that out of our society could come a Jim Robinson; all of us can be proud of the work he has done.

I commend this book to my fellow-citizens—of all the nations.

CROSSROADS PROJECTS IN AFRICA – 1961

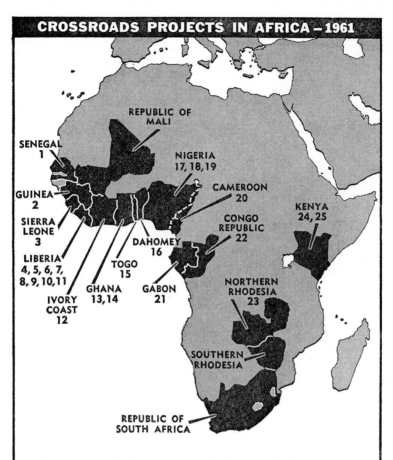

REPUBLIC OF MALI

SENEGAL
1

GUINEA
2

SIERRA LEONE
3

LIBERIA
4, 5, 6, 7,
8, 9, 10, 11

IVORY COAST
12

GHANA
13, 14

TOGO
15

DAHOMEY
16

NIGERIA
17, 18, 19

CAMEROON
20

GABON
21

CONGO REPUBLIC
22

NORTHERN RHODESIA
23

KENYA
24, 25

SOUTHERN RHODESIA

REPUBLIC OF SOUTH AFRICA

1. Popenguine—school
2. Mamou—youth hostel
3. Magburaka—lorry park
4. Robertsport—teaching center
5. Monrovia—teaching center
6. Buchanan—teaching center
7. Greenville—teaching center
8. Gbaranga—teaching center
9. Harper—teaching center
10. Bomi Hills—teaching center
11. Zorzor—teaching center
12. Abidjan—school
13. Nkwatia—school
14. Papayebre—model village
15. Womé—school
16. Porto Novo—two schools
17. Lagos—road work
18. Sapele—youth hostel
19. Achina—stairs to well
20. Guzang—maternity center
21. Libreville—science research center
22. Mouyandzi—youth hostel
23. Kitwe—amphitheater
24. Nairobi—road to clinic
25. Nairasha—YMCA

OPERATION CROSSROADS AFRICA

1

Kitwe

"WITH ONE STROKE I JUST ABOUT FINISHED YOUR BOOK THEN, Mrs. Plimpton!"

I looked up from shoveling to investigate that provocative remark. A pickax had been arrested about a foot over my head, and the bearded youth astride the ditch had just missed killing me. Absorbed in ditch-digging, I had unwittingly backed into the range of a pickax wielded by one of the Crossroaders.

This was the comedy of errors the Africans had been expecting. They had been looking on dumfounded at the sight of Americans working with their hands; their wonder was intensified by the presence of black and white people working together, and the fact that girls were sharing in the work with the men. I had felt a slight conflict at posing as an American woman shoveling out a ditch, until I thought back to the last snowy winter in Amherst, Massachusetts, and realized the image wasn't entirely inaccurate. Only the substance in the shovel was different. Instead of clearing a driveway of snow in the United States, we were digging out the tenth row of seats for an amphitheater in Kitwe, Northern Rhodesia. The site for the amphitheater was an old anthill, and

1

the ground was as hard as frozen snow. The boys were pickaxing the resistant soil while the girls shoveled the loosened dirt into wheelbarrows. Everyone kept counting the rows already dug. There were three more to go before proceeding to the next stage of mixing cement and pouring it into the ditches to form the necessary thirteen rows of benches.

The amphitheater was not an entirely typical kind of Crossroads project, since it was being constructed for the Mindola Ecumenical Center, which is unique in all Africa. Kitwe is an immensely wealthy, ten-year-old town, a by-product of Nklana Copper Mines (third largest in the world), where European laborers have enjoyed a high standard of living, and Africans have been exposed to a better life but denied its privileges. Fear has haunted this country where 66,000 defensive Europeans have controlled the fate of 2,360,000 resentful Africans. In 1957 a Congregational minister called Peter Matthews came from Australia to Kitwe to investigate the possibilities for a new approach to these tensions. He founded the Mindola Ecumenical Center as a neutral haven where groups of people formerly not on speaking terms could meet and discuss their many disagreements. The amphitheater was planned for such conferences. The work project had already become a meeting place for Africans, coloreds, Europeans, and a joking, singing, hard-working group of Crossroaders that held both charm and curiosity for the people of Kitwe. They would pass by to observe and question the Crossroaders, and then become interested enough to join in the work. Almost two hundred people representing various sections of the Copper Belt Society participated in this project by the end of the summer. Many of my photographs are of Crossroaders leaning on their shovels or pickaxes, deep in conversation. I have to explain to those who feel a work project should portray only physical action that these were the unofficial conferences at Kitwe.

The morning after my arrival the Crossroaders were putting in their hour's work before breakfast when two African boys came strolling along the path which led to town from the nearby mineworkers' compound. One of them stopped, and we heard him remark to the other, "Who are those people?"

"They can't be Europeans working like that. But they are white."

"Maybe they're American Europeans."

Luke, one of the African students working on the project with us, was pushing a loaded wheelbarrow precariously along one of the aisles between the ditches. He called over to the Africans standing on the path, "These are just plain Americans— nothing European about them. They like to work. Come down and talk to them."

They wandered closer and examined Don Harris. "You African?" they asked.

Don replied, "No, I'm not an African, I'm an American Negro. My ancestors were African."

"Are you coming back to live in Africa?"

Don said, "No, I've just come with Crossroads for the summer."

"Why don't the American Negroes come back to live in Africa?" they asked.

"America is our home now," Don said, "just the way it is for the people who've moved there from England and France and all those other countries."

"Oh," said the Africans. "What tribe do you belong to?"

"We don't have different tribes in the United States."

"What language do the American Negroes talk?"

"Everyone speaks English in the United States. It is the one language for all of us."

The Africans exchanged glances of wonder. "You didn't come over here with all those white men, did you?"

Don nodded.

"Are you working for them?"

"Goodness, no," said Don. "We're all working together. I happen to be the only Negro in this group, but most of the other groups of Operation Crossroads Africa have several Negroes."

The Africans looked in wonder. "We have never heard of white men and black men living and working together like this before. It is amazing! Where are the other Crossroads groups?"

"There are sixteen other groups working in eleven other countries in Africa," Don said. "Many of them are building schools. We are building an amphitheater."

Several more Africans had joined the group around Don by now, and the other Crossroaders had moved in too.

One of the Africans asked, "Did the government send you people here?"

Another Crossroader answered, "No, it is completely independent of the government."

"Are you—what do they call it—Peace Corps?"

Tom Hoeber explained. "Many people confuse us with the Peace Corps. Operation Crossroads Africa was a kind of forerunner to the Peace Corps in Africa, but they are entirely separate. You see, the Peace Corps is run by the government and Crossroads is a private organization. Operation Crossroads Africa brings students over just for the summer, while the Peace Corps program is for two years. It is an introduction to Africa for us. We come to learn about you and see your country."

"Will the Peace Corps bring over Americans like you?"

"Yes, they will be young people very much like ourselves who want to help you develop your country. Some of us may join the Peace Corps when we have finished college."

"If the government doesn't send you, who pays you for coming?"

"Ah," said Tom, "we ourselves pay for the privilege of coming to your country."

"What! You pay to come and dig ditches for us in Africa? How much does it cost you to come?"

Tom explained that it cost $1700 to send every student for the summer, and that Crossroads puts up $800 and each student pays $900.

"Where does your organization get the money?"

"From foundations, colleges, churches, and individuals."

The African said, "You must be very rich yourself to pay nine hundred dollars to come here."

The other Crossroaders chimed in. "No, we're not rich. We all took jobs in the States to earn enough money to come to Africa."

Tom added, "Last summer I had two jobs—working eighty hours a week in all, and last winter when I was studying at Wesleyan College I had jobs washing dishes and selling books. All these jobs helped pay for my trip."

Ron Fleming broke in. "Diana and I go to Pomona College. The whole college pitched in to send five of us on Crossroads this summer."

Tom said, "Hundreds of people in the United States and Canada have made our coming possible because they are interested in Africa."

The Africans could hardly believe it. "You mean all these people volunteer—they care about us and our country?"

"Exactly! They can't all come to Africa to get to know you, but they send us and we go back and tell them all we have learned."

Luke said, "The Crossroaders know us Africans better than the white people who have lived here all their lives. They talk to people everywhere. They really seem to care about us. They have even learned some Bemba."

One of the Africans asked, "Did you say there are Crossroaders from Canada too?"

James Stockton said, "Ken Woods and I are from Canada. The Board of Men of the United Church of Canada sent us. A group of people in the city of Hamilton, Ontario, became so interested in what we were doing that they raised a thousand dollars to help pay for the supplies to build the amphitheater."

"Are many of you sent by Protestant church groups?"

John Landry said, "James is studying to be a Protestant minister, but I am Catholic and Sue Gumpert here is Jewish. We represent all religions. I am a cadet on leave from West Point. One-third of my class applied to come on Crossroads, but they could take only three of us. It's been great for me because I come from Florida where I never had a chance to know any Negroes."

"How did you girls get the money to come?" an African asked.

Cindie Chutter said, "One-third of mine was a Crossroads scholarship, one-third was earned washing dishes and baby-sitting while I was at Smith College, and my family helped out with the rest."

The Africans found it hard to believe that these American and Canadian Crossroaders represented so many other people who had volunteered to help with this project in Africa. It would have been much easier to understand if they had been ordered to do it by the government.

One of the Africans asked me, "What are you doing here? Are you some sort of leader?"

I explained that Reverend Hugh Nelson and his wife were the leaders and that I was just visiting for a few days. I planned to visit fourteen of the seventeen Crossroads groups in hopes of writing a book about them.

"How did Operation Crossroads Africa get started?" they asked.

"An American Negro minister first got the idea and interested others. His name is Reverend James H. Robinson. He and his wife plan to visit you later this summer."

2

Robinson

OPERATION CROSSROADS AFRICA SPRANG LIKE A BRANCH OUT OF THE
life of James H. Robinson. The name "Robinson" did not grow
on his proverbial family tree; his grandfather picked it from the
kindest of the three masters for whom he was a slave. Robinson's
family lived in the "Bottoms," which described the depth of the
lowest part of Knoxville, Tennessee, morally and economically.
The environment of his childhood was as bad as any that our
country has to offer.

A tributary creek of the Tennessee River ran through the
Bottoms. Every spring, when the Smoky Mountains thawed, the
Tennessee River would back up into the creek, and the flood
waters would creep up the brick stilts of the Robinsons' shack
past the wading stage, and seriously threaten a disanchoring. As
the water seeped through the floorboards, the Robinson children
would make a wet withdrawal to their beds. There they would
remain—shivering, starved, and frightened—until the floods sub-
sided. One slight compensation for these miseries was the temporary absence of stench from the outhouses and nearby slaughter-
houses, where Robinson's father worked. His father blamed the

floods on God, and James felt as if he hated God for sending the floods, which not only destroyed life and property, but left the Bottoms ridden with disease.

Robinson's father was an ardent member of the Sanctified Church and a product of its fire-thunder-and-flood variety of religion. He spent most of his spare time praying and reading the Bible; and even when his family was starving he still contributed to the Church. He made his six children attend church twice a week and three times on Sunday. The children resented the way the church dominated their father, and they feared their father's domination over them. He often whipped them without provocation.

There were knocks to take on every side. When they delivered wash to the "white folks" for their hard-working mother, they would have to fight off abusive white boys on the way. When they returned home, covered with cuts and bruises, their father would give them a follow-up lashing as a punishment for defending themselves. He believed that his boys should accept it as their fate to be persecuted and hated by white people all their lives. This attitude infuriated Robinson. He was too angry to have his spark snuffed out like the other Negroes in the Bottoms, and his own wrath served to fan his inner fire and strengthen his convictions.

James H. Robinson knew he was just as good as any white man, and his mother was the one person who reaffirmed his belief. She listened with compassion to his every desire. She never despaired like his father, but always supported his dreams for a better life. In times of trouble she encouraged his flights of fancy from the rugged realities they were all facing. Robinson describes how during the floods "she would huddle us about her and make us forget the chill and unrelenting hunger. She told us stories of the knights of old, the slave revolts and the Indians of the Smoky Mountains. When our courage flagged there would be a new tale to fire and kindle our imaginations. For a moment at least, the shabby room became the great hall of a palace, and the rocker in which she sat a chariot drawn by magnificent steeds. My sisters were princesses, my brother was a prince, and of course, I the king."*

Indeed, he was later to become king of many situations in life, creating the very kingdoms of which he was the natural sovereign. Crossroads was only one of them.

The first move up from the Bottoms and into the world outside of Knoxville was to Ohio. Robinson's family moved to Youngstown when he was about fourteen, and then to Cleveland. Although he left the spring floods behind, he did not shed his other problems. There was no escape from poverty. He took what jobs he could after school, working in clubs and restaurants, bowling alleys, barber shops, and scrap heaps. Although the preferential jobs were reserved for white people, he learned to respect the dignity of any type of labor. "No man ever soiled his heart by soiling his hands," was a belief of his which was later to become a characteristic of Crossroads.

His constant need to work at odd jobs left precious little time for studying. Pursuing his education entailed one obstacle after another, and at times the demands on him seemed overwhelming. When his mother died of tuberculosis at the age of thirty-two, he lost his only source of encouragement. Shortly afterward, he acquired a stepmother who was the antithesis of his own mother. She encouraged his father to oppose and ridicule his burning desire for an education. Seven times his father withdrew him from school because he thought education for Negroes was useless. James was finally forced to leave home in order to continue his schooling, and as a result on many a night he slept shivering in vestibules. He was always hungry. He never had enough to eat until he was eighteen and got a job in the kitchen of Lincoln University.

More piercing than all the pains of hunger and cold during these schooldays were the hurts of the heart. Whenever he brushed close to a white man he suffered another thorn. How could he establish a sense of human dignity when around every corner of

* James H. Robinson, *Road Without Turning*, p. 38.

life there was a white man to turn him back? At that time he hated white people with all but the tiniest corner of his heart. He was boiling with revenge.

Revenge has no safety valves. Gang warfare provided the opportunity for Robinson and his young friends to uncork some of their pent-up hostility against their white oppressors. His gang might have been a bunch of wholesome, crazy kids if they had had an even chance at being normal teen-agers. They reacted the way any high-spirited boys would if stepped on by the heavy boots of segregation; they kicked back, as hard as they could, whenever they could. After having the satisfaction of beating up some white boys, Robinson began to realize that there was no happiness in such physical revenge. Beneath his rebellious impulses lay a truly gentle spirit. He was revolted by seeing anyone really hurt.

It was in the world of books that he discovered a more acceptable form of revenge. Robinson read incessantly—any book he could get hold of. He discovered that intellectually he could wrestle successfully with anyone. His facile learning ability and vivid self-expression won him respect. The waves of self-respect brought about a turning of the internal tide, and his desire for revenge gradually ebbed. His reading also opened doors of understanding to himself and others. It occurred to him that white people suppressed Negroes not because they were really superior but because even they were insecure human beings. His growing contacts with individuals who expressed concern rather than hostility for Negroes led him to believe that white people were not all alike any more than Negroes were. To his surprise, he began to realize that he could no longer hold his hate. Although he had every excuse to identify solely with the Negro cause, his heart was too big for "Negroes only."

With his increasing self-respect, Robinson became more aware of his own unique potentialities. His groping for a religious faith had been as difficult as his search for security in society; they were somewhat related. Although he had been familiar with the Bible since childhood, he had to work out his own interpretation. He had wanted desperately to believe in God, but he could not square the rote religion forced upon him with the circumstances of his life. He began to doubt that there could be a God who would do anything about the depravity of Knoxville, the poverty of his family, and most of all, the treatment of Negroes by white Christians. He could not accept the idea of a punishing God or a society of non-communicating black and white people.

Rather than serving as a deterrent to his belief in God, his early doubts sharpened the search and strengthened the eventual find. It was a long time before he discovered any illustrations in life which could serve to make real the long passages from the Bible that he had been made to memorize as a child. One particular verse especially became an important reality: God "did not leave Himself without witness" (Acts, 14:17). In classrooms he was meeting teachers, in books philosophers, in kitchens housewives, and in fields laborers whose lives bore witness to the fact that there must be a God. He began to discover more and more possibilities for putting a very practical religion into action. The ministry was the best field for developing these possibilities.

When he decided to enter the ministry he was still faced with the all but insurmountable problems of financing a higher education. After a year at Western Reserve, he was informed by a Presbyterian minister that if he joined his church there would be a scholarship for a young man like himself interested in the clergy. With this support he transferred to Lincoln University. But even with a small scholarship and innumerable jobs, it was hard scraping.

During one of his many moments of financial despair, a fairy godmother appeared on the scene. Lorraine Miller was a teacher from Tonawanda, New York, where, around the turn of the century, the entire Negro population had been driven out and not allowed to return. Miss Miller felt compelled to atone for the sins of her fellow white people. At the time, she did not know Robinson, but she had heard of his earnest desire to get an education. Despite her meager salary she underwrote the last three years of his college education, enabling him to remain at Lincoln University. More important than the change that took place in his pockets was the change that was taking place in his heart. Miss Miller was one more example that "God did not leave Himself without witness."

Robinson went to Lincoln University filled with controversial ideas, and debating provided a good means of testing some of them. It was not long before he proved his ability to hold a multitude of people spellbound. He was chosen class valedictorian. He took every advantage of his opportunities and became an expert at the very thing he had once been forbidden—communicating with all kinds of people. It is this ability which has not only brought him close to so many Crossroaders, but has served as an example for them in realizing their own potentialities to contact others.

The very power of his words provoked fear as well as admiration. His oratorical skills, while enriching his life, were also endangering it. During his summer vacations from Lincoln University he took preaching jobs in Southern churches, and became so influential in stirring people to action on behalf of the Negro cause that he was almost lynched.

One night he was alone in the church. He heard the jeering mob come marching up the street. He looked for an exit, but the crowd was too close. The time was too late to think of a way out. He froze in the doorway, prey prepared for the beasts. A car honked and hurried ahead of the mob. It halted abruptly in front of the church. A strange white man jumped out and grabbed at the victim. He shoved Robinson with haste into his auto. White man and black man drove into the night. They drove on and on till they came to a bus stop. Robinson got out, and the driver departed. Robinson was right: white men were not all alike.

Negroes are not all alike either. Robinson refused to let adversity get the upper hand and work as a handicap in his life. The very obstacles of his life seemed to serve as a sort of spiritual fitness course for the special kind of leadership for which he was destined

—leadership of black and white people. Robinson's ability as a leader was significantly recognized when he went to Union Theological Seminary in New York. There he was unanimously elected president of his class.

His first real kingdom for creative leadership was in Harlem. As soon as he graduated from Union Theological Seminary, he founded the Church of the Master, with his first congregation consisting of four adults and six children. Under his leadership it grew to three thousand men, women, and children of different races. To do justice to all the activities which developed in connection with the church would need a book in itself.

As one inspiration led to another, Operation Crossroads Africa developed from one of the many projects of the Church of the Master. It has become his major interest, and he has recently resigned from the Church of the Master to give Crossroads his undivided attention.

Along with his strenuous schedule of social service in Harlem, he found time to speak at many schools and colleges across the country. Possessed of a magic key for unlocking students, he has helped thousands of white and Negro students to find themselves as vital Americans. Many young people have become drowsy with the condition of complacency inherent in our so-called "privileged" American lives. They want to know more, feel more, and do more about the world they live in. More than one white student has said, "I envy the Negro—he has something so definite to fight for in life." What is enviable is the unleashing of strong, dedicated feelings. Robinson knows the secret combination which reaches these students, and he is an artist at tapping their strengths.

One of the colleges he has visited frequently is Amherst. In the spring of 1941 when he came to speak he was troubled over a recent crime wave in Harlem which had been given exaggerated publicity in the newspapers. Who could better understand these teen-agers and their desire for revenge than he who had experienced the same causes for rebellion in his youth? And who could care more that these disillusioned young people be given the opportunity for productive lives? Robinson didn't have notes or a prepared speech when he talked to the Amherst men that night. He just spoke what was in his heart. At such moments he has ways of captivating his audience completely. His round, jocular expression is reminiscent of a famous character "laying a finger aside of his nose." With half-closed eyes he can move them through a Shakespearean cycle of emotions. With earnestness and humor he agitates them into heated protest and then suggests a possible course of action. After Robinson had shared his feelings about delinquency in Harlem with the Amherst students that night, they were not ready to let him go. They flocked around him like seagulls agitating after a returning fishing boat. "What can we do to help?" they kept asking.

"Well . . ." He did have an answer. Just a few days before, he had received an offer of a 470-acre farm in Winchester, New Hampshire, for an interracial children's camp. This land might make it possible for children to get away from hot, tense Harlem for a summer's vacation, but there were no camp buildings. He told the Amherst students about it. That night twenty-five men volunteered to help build a camp. They were soon joined by Smith and Mount Holyoke girls. A tradition was started by which students from many colleges went to Winchester for week ends in the spring and fall to help build Rabbit Hollow Camp for boys (and later Lake Forest Camp for girls). Fifteen hundred students volunteered to work on these projects—four or five times as many as Robinson could use. This overwhelming response and success gave encouragement to the thought that what works at home may also work abroad.

In 1951 the Board of Foreign Missions of the Presbyterian Church visited Rabbit Hollow. They were so impressed with what had been accomplished that they were prompted to explore the possibilities of similar youth movements abroad. They chose Robinson as their emissary to go on a six-month exploratory tour through Europe, Africa, and Asia. He visited over a dozen countries, made hundreds of speeches, and talked to thousands of people.

In 1954 he went on a second, more concentrated tour of Africa. Again Robinson lived with the people and talked to them everywhere by the thousands. He contacted many African leaders. After making these innumerable and varied contacts, he came to the conclusion that "Although the people of Asia and Africa have serious questions about us and sometimes are not convinced that we mean what we say, they are nevertheless motivated by precisely the same sociological, economic, political, and nationalistic drives that have motivated our own nation. They earnestly want to believe in us and they want our friendship and our help. They also want security, freedom, and the right to determine their own destiny in their own way, but in cooperation with the rest of the world. They are willing to listen to what both we and the Communists have to say. Asians and Africans are in precarious suspension, with their millions as yet uncommitted. The pendulum can swing either way. The hour is late and there is not much time." *

As he waited for a plane to leave Liberia that summer, Robinson was feeling particularly aware of the lateness of the hour. Plane connections were extremely difficult; one could wait weeks for the desired flight. Robinson's enforced waiting at Roberts Field gave him extra time to think. What significant thing could Americans do in Africa? His mind kept wandering back to the enthusiastic students who had volunteered so eagerly to help out at Rabbit Hollow. They had expressed such intense pleasure after building something useful with their hands. They had experienced the *esprit de corps* that arises among people who work on a project together. Africans and Americans would need the aid of just such a bond to counteract their many differences. Was it too much of

* James H. Robinson, *Tomorrow Is Today*, p. 16.

a dream to imagine American students working with African students to build an African counterpart of Rabbit Hollow? His imagination was always ready for a take-off.

His reverie was interrupted by the sound of an engine at the other end of Roberts Field. Robinson inquired, to discover that this was a private German plane. There were others. The German pilots were camping on the edge of the air field close to their planes. They were there for the express purpose of taking anyone anywhere at any time. "Where do you want to go?" This was too good to be true. What a contrast to the delay and frustration caused by the inadequate scheduled flights! Robinson became inspired by the German pilots who were living so simply on the spot with a relaxed readiness to serve. Couldn't American youth take a page out of this German book? This was the way for young Americans to come to Africa—not as pilots of airplanes, but as pilots for goodness-knows-what movement to involve the emerging generation of Americans in the emerging countries of Africa. They could live in African villages with the same kind of relaxed readiness for service. They could work on a project—probably not a camp like Rabbit Hollow, but more likely a school, or perhaps a church, or whatever was most needed in a particular village. Robinson's dreams for Operation Crossroads Africa were gradually taking shape on the sunny airstrip of Liberia.

Robinson returned to the United States fired with his plans for Crossroads. He started corresponding with African leaders to try to discover whether they would be in favor of such a program. Would African students want American students to come and live, work, and play with them? The response was positive. Students in the United States listened to his ideas with equal enthusiasm. He talked to many American leaders, but he had difficulty in getting their support in 1954. He talked with people everywhere, and the general reaction was discouraging: "Who on earth would want to go and live in an African village when they could go on a safari?" For three years he contended with this kind of apathy.

During these three years he was also working on another

African project. His travels had made him aware of the intellectual isolation of Africa. Deploring their dearth of books, he organized a book drive throughout the United States called Books for Democracy.

Robinson traveled all over the United States appealing for books and talking about Africa. The process of collecting the books was as educational for the Americans as the receiving was for the Africans. Robinson was one of the first people in this country to re-evaluate the old concept of "dark Africa," and he emphasized that the "darkest" thing about Africa was the American ignorance of that continent. Always in the background of these talks was his hope of interesting people eventually in the possibilities of an Operation Crossroads Africa. The immediate result of his efforts was the collection of a half million books, which were shipped free by Farrell Lines to Kenya, Uganda, Southern Rhodesia, Nigeria, Liberia, and Sierra Leone.

In the spring of 1957 Robinson was at a religious conference at Occidental College in Pasadena, California. He did not talk about Africa until the very end of the conference, but what he had to say electrified the students. Afterward, they gathered around him, asking him questions. He talked with them for quite a while before retiring to his hotel room. At one-thirty there was a knock on his door, and he got up to find a group of students standing outside. They were too stimulated for sleep, so why should they allow it to their stimulator? He had only given six speeches the day before. Never too weary when really needed, he got up and talked with the students for the rest of the night. He had planned to fly home the next morning, but his life was no longer his own. The campus was already plastered with posters reading "Come to the bowl to hear Robinson at 1:30." He was forced to cancel his flight and postpone his return.

As a result of this encounter, the students raised $15,000 to send ten students to Africa the following summer. That summer three hundred students, who had summer jobs, volunteered two days' pay each toward the project. They approached any possible donor, even persuading Nixon and Stevenson to contribute $500 each. They organized an African Studies Course at UCLA with enough paying adults enrolled to make it possible for students to attend free. Every Friday night they brought in African students to speak to them. They wrote to other possible groups to encourage similar activities. This self-propelled group was the handful that started Crossroads.

In 1958 fifty-nine Americans and one Canadian went to French Cameroon, Ghana, Liberia, Nigeria, and Sierra Leone. The first Crossroads expedition was an experiment in every sense of the word. No one had any idea how this pilot project was going to work or whether it could be continued. It was planned entirely by correspondence. An extra supply of faith was needed on every side, and it was a miracle that everything worked out as well as it did. But the value of the work project as a medium for introducing Americans and Africans to one another was well proven.

This trial summer also pointed up the need for lots of planning and preparation before expanding the project. The year 1959 was spent in just such planning. Members of the Crossroads staff went over to Africa to study possibilities for the next summer. There was a great advantage in planning the projects directly with the African leaders. In 1960 one hundred and eighty-three Crossroaders went to ten countries. To the original five were added five more French countries: Togo, Dahomey, Ivory Coast, Guinea, and Senegal. These emphasized the need and importance for real knowledge of the French language.

In 1961 two hundred and twenty Crossroaders went to fourteen countries, Kenya, Gabon, Republic of Congo, and Northern Rhodesia being added to the ten of the year before. There were two groups in Ghana and three in Nigeria, making a total of seventeen groups. Two boys from one of the Ghana groups were even sent down to a World Council Ecumenical Work Camp in the Union of South Africa for the summer.

Crossroads could not succeed without someone's untiring attention to the thousands of details which make the great original ideas work. Doctor Robinson is very lucky in having a wife with a sublime sense of organization, not only for big things but for the little things that make the big ones possible. Anyone who enters the Crossroads office at 150 Fifth Avenue in New York City is aware of the magic hand of the First Lady of Crossroads.

Operation Crossroads Africa offers quite a new approach to our foreign policy, but there are some understandable questions as to the value of such a project.

3

Questions

"WHY SPEND ALL SUMMER DOING BY HAND WHAT COULD BE DONE in a few days by a couple of efficient machines?" This is not an unusual question posed to Crossroaders. The answer is that bulldozers neither ask nor answer questions; dump trucks neither laugh nor sing; electric drills make a big racket, but they can't communicate. *People* still have something machines don't have. Crossroads is more concerned with that "something" than with the expediency of the machine. The primary purpose of a Crossroads work project is not the speedy finishing of a concrete building, but the gradual beginning of an intangible bridge between very different people. A mysterious bond develops between people who pool their efforts in a joint enterprise of physical labor. It is more elemental than an intellectual exchange, and has a strong emotional component. The same thing holds true between grownups and children too young for intellectual communication. Nothing in words could substitute for the contact made by their building together a sand castle or whittling a small wooden boat.

"Why not give all the money that it takes to send the Crossroaders to Africa directly to the Africans?" is a question the

Africans sometimes ask. In our foreign policy we have specialized in sending aid, in exporting equipment, and in building roads and dams and embassies. And at home we have presented our children with fantastic toys from F. A. O. Schwarz and written "Lots of love" on the cards at Christmas. The jeeps, planes, and ships for other countries were sent with "lots of love" too. Somehow none of these things have come off quite the way we wanted them to, and it's hard to understand what could have gone wrong. Our sophisticated acts of good did not impart the simple message that *we care*. We have specialized in meetings with very different people in glamorous settings, yet we seem to be the most misunderstood nation on earth. We have begun to feel like a wallflower in the world ballroom. Although we've put our best foot forward, we have missed out on some of the basic steps of good communication with other people.

The work project was devised primarily as a means of communication. It seems to be the most effective method of breaking down all the cultural and racial barriers. Whether by digging a ditch or mixing cement, very different people are suddenly given the opportunity to work hard together in an informal setting. They need the security of sharing something real before they can explore their cultural, political, and philosophical differences. Understanding grows out of the exploration, and from understanding comes friendship. Crossroaders have been amazed at what similarities they have discovered between Africans and Americans. The differences have been only a veneer.

Those who are not aware that primarily the value of a Crossroads work project is a *means* and who tend to evaluate only the *end* architectural accomplishment ask, "What possible good could those minute cement creations do in vast, vast Africa?" Maybe they do seem like the proverbial "grains of sand" when you think of the mighty land. However, wherever one small schoolhouse or clinic has been erected, no matter how architecturally modest, something very significant has been added that wasn't there before.

Many people have brought up the question, "Why bring labor

to Africa when that is what they have most of?" If their greatest need is education, "Why don't we devote all our efforts to teaching?" One of the biggest obstacles to overcome before Americans can have an honest relationship with Africans, and before black and white people anywhere can enjoy a natural rapport, is the stigma of the master-subject relationship. We have inherited the attitudes created by years of colonial supremacy in Africa. The idea of equality will remain purely theoretical, even in the independent African countries, until actual experience has contradicted the more familiar pattern of relationship of superiority and inferiority. Although the ideal teacher-pupil relationship is one of mutual exchange, the Africans are familiar only with the concept of a superior teacher and inferior pupil. Therefore the teacher-pupil situation does not provide the kind of therapy which a work project offers so naturally.

"What are those pretty girls doing with wheelbarrows instead of teaching child care?" the Nairobi newspapers wanted to know. The idea of girls on a work project mystifies many people. "What do the girls do, anyway?" The answer is that they work along with the boys, within their physical limitations. Obviously eight boys could dig more ditches and lay more bricks in one day than four boys and four girls, but without the girls the work projects would not be nearly so gay. The girls provide a certain something that road gangs simply don't have. Also, the girls have a special opportunity to get to know the sometimes hard-to-reach African women who suffer from a double sense of inferiority in being women as well as black. All the more important is the fact that our girls do not breeze in like visions from Hollywood, with "instructions" on how to counteract years of African domestic experience. No African woman would believe that an American woman can also work unless she saw it with her own eyes. And work means physical labor for the African woman. Once she experiences a feeling of equality with an American, her shyness recedes, and she is able to discuss some of the problems which beset her household today.

The question some of the foundations are asking is, "Why do we need a private organization like Crossroads, now that we have the Peace Corps?" Crossroads and the Peace Corps serve very different purposes. Private and public enterprises are as important complementing one another overseas as they are at home. The Peace Corps carries the privileges, responsibilities, and limitations inherent in any governmental organization. Crossroads has the independence of a private institution. It is freer to move. The students who join the Peace Corps are making a two-year commitment. Crossroads gives a student an introduction to Africa during one summer vacation, without compromising his long-term plans. The Crossroads experience serves to help the individual make decisions about his future commitments.

The Peace Corps represents the United States government in Africa. The Africans have not experienced our form of democratic government. For them it is a new idea that a government can really represent the spontaneous will of the people. Crossroads is in a more advantageous position to impart the message that the people of America care about the people of Africa. The very fact that Crossroads is entirely financed by voluntary donations of individuals interested in Africa is the most convincing argument in African terms, for it appeals to their community tribal spirit. Crossroads and Peace Corps have no reason to operate in competition with one another. They have different kinds of opportunity to express the same American ideal.

There are many questions and many answers in preparing Crossroaders to go to Africa. For every Crossroader the exciting moment comes when he can make way for his own fresh impressions, and tuck away all the questions and answers by others.

4

Washington—
Send-off

A VIVACIOUS BLONDE IN A PINK LINEN SHEATH WAS CELEBRATING HER twentieth birthday. The lights were vibrant in the National Cathedral and there was a contagious vitality in the gathering of people. It was the final meeting of the Crossroaders before their departure for Africa, a most diverse group of young people, who had become acquainted during the past week of orientation in Washington. Although they came from all over the United States and Canada and were chosen to represent different religious, racial, and economic backgrounds, the purpose they shared gave them an air of unity and distinction. There was a general sense of restlessness and anticipation among them. They were saturated with good advice and eager to try out their own inexperienced selves on this great African adventure.

They knew they were lucky to be chosen. Doctor Robinson had told them, "Seven times your number wanted to come."

They knew they were to be representative. Robert Ehrman, speaking for the United States Information Service, had told them,

"You are going to be what the United States says America is. You're it."

They knew they were envied. Harris Wofford, representing the Peace Corps, had said, "We salute you. We envy you."

They knew they would have ups and downs. Harold Isaacs, who had made a study for the Massachusetts Institute of Technology on the 1960 group of Crossroaders, warned them of a pattern of exhilaration followed by frustration before they settled down realistically in their new environment.

They knew they might come down with malaria if they forgot to take their aralen pills, or failed to cover their bare spots with "OFF" after dark, or failed to drape their mosquito netting over their cots at night. They might contract schistosomiasis if they went barefoot or swam in any fresh waters. If they failed to boil their drinking water they could get typhoid, for the inoculations provided only a partial protection. They might also domicile pin worms, round worms, or tape worms from unclean food-handlers or uncooked food. And if they worried too much about any of these possible ailments they might suffer the symptoms even if they didn't catch the actual disease. Dr. Sylvester Carter, the Crossroads consultant, had humorously warned them of all these possibilities.

They knew they would have to "play it by ear" and "expect the unexpected." All the old Crossroaders had told them that.

They also had begun to realize that now more than ever they were going to have to think for themselves. They had implored Christopher Thoron, the representative of the United Nations, to give them an acceptable answer they could pull out of their pockets like a handkerchief any time an African challenged them about Cuba. All they could get from him was, "Your answer is as good as mine."

The Reverend Francis Sayre, Jr., had made it possible for them to use the Cathedral School building as their orientation headquarters all week and to meet in the Cathedral that night. G. Mennen Williams had just finished his message from the State Department to the Crossroaders when Doctor Robinson introduced the birthday girl in the pink linen sheath. She was Adele Smith from Chicago, studying at Radcliffe. She had been chosen as spokesman for the Crossroaders that night before departure. They had listened all week; how did they feel?

Adele answered:

"Each of us has his own individual reasons for being here tonight, for, as we have found in the past few days, we are all very different. Yet despite these differences most of us have at least one trait in common—foresight. Last November we had the foresight to consider where we wanted to be in seven months. We were looking for something exciting, something challenging, something novel. But we wanted more than an adventure—we wanted to do something significant, something directly related to our rapidly changing world. We were seeking experience in the developing areas where these changes are striking and profound. For this reason Africa appealed.

"There are some of us who before last November were already immersed in African studies, who will be using this summer as a basis for further intensive research, who will see for themselves the country and the people about which we have been reading. We could have gone as tourists, but the curious tourist has none of the opportunity we will have to talk to Africans and to overcome the natural suspicion that any person bears toward any intruding foreigner. We, however, equipped with 'frisbies,' balloons, and shovels, are prepared to share in a specific project with the Africans. This gives our presence a certain legitimacy and gives the Africans an opportunity to reciprocate our friendship. Some will, some won't. But our chances for developing successful and genuine personal relationships with another people are certainly greater than those of any tourist.

"We have been told a frustrating number of times to 'expect the unexpected' and not to 'save' Africa. Convinced of this, we are going to learn about Africa and its people. With varying degrees of patience, we are waiting for a chance to prove ourselves. We hope that, while we are learning by living with the Africans, the Africans themselves will learn—learn what twelve American students are like, what these students who have no direct responsibility to their government feel about their country. We must defend our country where defense is valid with lucid explanations of the problem; yet we must not hesitate to criticize where criticism is deserved. We will have an opportunity to show the Africans what we believe, to follow up our words with deeds, for much of what we say will be tested in daily life. More important than advocating integration is demonstrating it. And it is especially in this area of racial relations that we will be questioned and watched very closely.

"Just as Africans have formed impressions and stereotypes of us, so we have formed images of the typical African. Three months is certainly time enough for us to dispel our preconceived notions, time enough for us to gain a limited understanding of the mores and motivations of another people. If we can recognize the similarities and respect the differences between ourselves and the particular group with which we will be working, perhaps we can accept more readily the differences between ourselves and the many other peoples of the world.

"When we return, we may be able to help other Americans understand some of the problems of a continent that had previously been only an abstraction to them. All of us will have chances to tell our friends of the experience, for it was in this informal manner that each of us heard about Crossroads.

"Many of us are idealistic, or we would not be here; all of us are naïve, for we are young. However, we think we know what we are getting into—though two months from now we surely will have different ideas. If our tents don't blow down in the middle of the worst rainstorm in fifty years, we will have little to joke about at parties. However, long hours and even longer days of waiting for essential materials are neither exciting nor amusing. They are trying and tedious. Yet we are all supposed to have some imagination, some initiative, and a sense of humor. If we employ these wisely, almost anything can be overcome, or endured.

"We have all spent time in preparation for the summer; we have done more than just appear at Washington at the appointed hour. The M.I.T. students here took time to negotiate with Mr. Land, who has, as a result, given the project eight Polaroid cameras. Some of us have spent time studying the language of the country—French or Swahili.

"Crossroads has asked each of us to pay nine hundred dollars of the total seventeen-hundred-dollar individual cost. For some this was easy. We handed the bill to our parents, who skeptically but willingly wrote a check. Hopefully, these people will recognize their fortunate positions and will continue to support Crossroads.

"Many of us, however, have undertaken numerous projects to raise money. The M.I.T. people made four hundred and fifty dollars showing a movie. Others have obtained term-time jobs; still others have arranged to sell articles to local newspapers. Appeals by letter, radio, and TV have been made to church groups and local clubs. The donations from these groups are numerous but very small, so raising money in this way requires persistence and optimism. Last year's Crossroaders have already accused this year's group of a lack of imagination, for apparently some of their more industrious women raised money giving twenty-five-cent back rubs. Most of the more serious undertakings are not easy; however, over sixty per cent of our group has raised money willingly. Crossroads, too, has been patient with those who have financial problems. They received numerous checks for one dollar and even one for fifty cents, and, as far as I know, managed to keep the record straight. Furthermore, when necessary, they have helped a few who could not be here unless their earnings had been supplemented.

"We are going to Africa, then, to learn about another people and about ourselves. We are doing something unusual, challenging, and politically significant. None of us will be able to look at the government buildings of every capital, but all of us will be able to work closely with a few select Africans, to gain an impression of what lies behind these symbolic buildings in their countries.

"There are many people who have made this year's project possible, but there is one man alone who is responsible for the existence of the entire program. We would like to express our thanks to Doctor Robinson, who conceived of Crossroads, who had the courage and persistence to make the project a reality, and whose ability to stimulate and work with people of all ages here and in Africa has made the program a success. We hope we will be worthy of the trust and confidence he has shown in us, that the 1961 Crossroaders will reinforce his belief in the value of his work."

Applause wouldn't have been proper in the Cathedral, but the enthusiasm of the whispers of Crossroaders filing out showed they were proud of their spokesman. She had expressed for many what was in their hearts.

The next time I saw the fresh, neat girl with ideas, in the pink linen dress, she was bronzed and grubby in blue jeans—the ideas put to action. Adele was one of the group to go to Kenya.

5

Kenya

WHEN YOU CAN JUST BARELY FIT YOUR LITTLE FINGER BETWEEN the Equator and Nairobi on a wall map of Africa, you wouldn't think the Crossroaders could need winter sleeping bags in July, but they were cold in their tents with the summer sleeping bags they'd brought along. Not nearly as conspicuous as the Equator on the map, but absolutely spectacular, are the Ngong Hills on one side and Mount Kenya on the other. There is a high-altitude sparkle in the air. In the chilly evenings the Crossroaders would sit between their tents on a circle of cinder blocks, their black and white faces shining in the light of a flickering fire. In the soft glow of the flames the articles of laundry strung on lines between the tents could no longer be identified. The silhouettes beyond suggested the flapping of giant elephant ears, for the leaves of the banana trees are never still. The sky had an unfamiliar look, as if the stars had been shuffled and redealt.

"*Sisi Tuasadiana*" was one of the songs the Crossroaders sang at night. It means "Let's help each other."

"*Tulimtuma Kenyatta Kwa uhuru
Tulimtuma Kenyatta*

30

Kenya, Uganda, Tanganyika,
Sisi tuasadiana."

The sentiment of the song was to send Kenyatta "to get freedom" and to combine independence with the federation of Kenya, Uganda, and Tanganyika; a happy union it would be if the governments were nearly as melodic as their names set to music. The Crossroaders had learned this popular political song from the African students who were living with them. The Radcliffe and Harvard students had studied Swahili the preceding winter, and the others were picking it up fast. Although it was possible to contact any of the educated Africans in English, it was even more important for the Crossroaders to show that they cared enough about the people to learn some of their language. A knowledge of the simplest greetings proved to be the greatest barrier-breaker. "*Jambo,*" meaning "Hi" in Swahili, was a good word to start with, and one could pass it back and forth like a football to anyone within reach.

Not every evening was spent around the campfire. Living so close to Nairobi, the Crossroaders were able to meet many people, both as a group and as individuals. The many-sided question as to when and how Kenya was to become independent has lots of spokesmen, and the Crossroaders knew representatives from about every angle of the debate. On one evening Jane might be discussing with Tom Mboya his problems as a member of the Legislative Council and General Secretary of KANU (Kenya African National Union), his hopes for an independent Kenya of Kenyans led by Kenyatta (all right for the Europeans to stay if they became equal citizens). Tim might be visiting a Kikuyu farmer in his mud hut in the village he had been forced to retreat to after the Mau Mau emergency of 1952. His greatest desire would be to get back to the fertile lands which his forefathers had once possessed and to which he had once had rights. David would often spend the evening down the road with Dr. Mungai Ngorge. The Crossroaders were camping next to his new clinic, and one of their work projects was to build an access road connecting the clinic with the main road. They were also terracing the land for showing films on health. Doctor Ngorge represented the real minority in Kenya— the precious minority of the professionally trained. How to enlarge this minority group is one of the biggest questions of all. Dick might well be passing the evening with the family of one of the Asian students. They had export-import problems, for the Indians are the traders of Kenya. Adele sometimes stayed overnight with some "white settlers" in a house with marble stairs, leopard rugs, and a swimming pool on the roof. She said that it was really true that some people slept with guns under their pillows. The newspapers carried warnings asking, "Is your gun safe?" for the owner would be fined if it was stolen. Part of the Mau Mau oath was to steal a white man's gun.

Other Crossroaders would be passing evenings with equally interesting people. Although it is sometimes difficult to maintain the unity of a group with such individual and varied contacts, there is a distinct advantage in the breadth of experience which comes from the sum total of such separate encounters. No one could feel that there was one simple solution to the many problems inherent in planning for an independent Kenya.

This was the first Crossroads group to come to Kenya, and they had not known what kind of a reception to expect. They found themselves in the dilemma of the child of divorced parents. The competing political parties were showering the Crossroaders with invitations, claiming credit for any Crossroad success, and disowning all Crossroaders in moments of trouble. This unexpected role was an exciting challenge, for it was important not to blunder. Their mistakes might ruin the chances for future Crossroaders in Kenya, and could even hurt the forthcoming Peace Corps.

There were many misconceptions and misunderstandings about the work project. The African planning committee had not anticipated these hard-working Americans. Europe had never volunteered such labor. Crossroaders were a peculiar new brand of white man. The project planned to occupy the Crossroaders for their first month was the clearing of a plot of land on which a library was to be built. The Crossroaders completed this job in exactly three days. The Africans hurriedly created other projects, none of which were very satisfying to the Crossroaders, who really wanted to build something. The whole concept of a work project as a method of really getting to know the Africans was new to the Kenyans. The newspapers gave it daily attention. One day the headlines would ask, "What are the Crossroaders doing in Kenya?" The next day the headlines would reply, "In defense of those Crossroads kids . . ." Fortunately, this was an articulate group, and they could hope that their answers to all the questions were convincing enough to pilot a course for better understanding of future Crossroaders.

For these extrovert Americans, listening was more difficult than talking. They had something to learn about how to detect subtle dissensions among the African students with whom they were sharing the work projects. They mistook politeness for general agreement on many of the details of living together. It was several weeks before the Crossroaders realized that the African students had been misled into believing that each Crossroader had a scholarship to America in his pocket which he would hand to any African student who chose to work long enough beside him. Both Africans and Americans were disillusioned when this misconception was finally aired. The Africans threatened to quit. After talking into the wee hours of the morning the Africans were persuaded not to leave the work project, and the Crossroaders felt that much had been gained by the recognition and resolution of this misunderstanding. Their advice to future Crossroaders arriving in Africa was to slip into the audience and encourage the less articluate Africans onto the stage so they could listen to African preconceived impressions of Americans before expressing themselves.

Besides all these kinds of Africans, there were the "white settlers" to think of. One Negro Crossroader said with real concern that he didn't think he *could* talk to a "white settler," he hated them so. My lack of personal experience with the deep hurts of exclusion made me feel inadequate to help. I was glad to be able to draw on the period in Robinson's life when he expressed frank hatred for all white people. How was he able to sublimate this feeling so that it didn't interfere with what he wanted most in life? Maybe the first step was recognizing the emotion. Crossroaders were of great help to one another in just talking over such feelings frankly. Later in the summer the same Negro Crossroader had occasion to talk with white settlers who were very insulting to him. His was the awful challenge of controlling his anger enough to act bigger than the people who were looking down on him.

The white Crossroaders also had to battle with their emotions, particularly in Kenya and the Rhodesias, where segregation was still a major problem. The wave of enthusiasm which had brought them to Africa had necessarily enlisted their greatest sympathy with its people, and the flow of identity between the Americans and the Africans caused the Europeans to appear sometimes narrow, although they were making many adjustments to integration more gracefully than our own Southerners.

One of my favorite Crossroaders in Kitwe, Northern Rhodesia, had very strong feelings for the Africans and a face that mirrored her every emotion. She looked beautiful while talking to some of the African leaders, but when she interviewed one of the managers of the Nklana Copper Mines she had a look of scorn which gave her every question a feeling of preconceived hostility. It is so easy to develop a new kind of haughtiness; being intolerant of intolerance can also be intolerant. Those who seem to have mismanaged their relationships with the Africans feel as guilty and defensive as a parent who suddenly becomes aware of the fact that he is responsible for a neglected child. Both need the chance to save face inconspicuously. It was important for the Crossroaders to realize that they did not need to sacrifice their friendship with the British (or French) because of their strong feelings toward the Africans. Also, there just might be something to learn. After all, none of us had ever taken a swing at absorbing 37,000 Africans from eighty different tribes with thirty different languages in a new mining town like Kitwe.

The Kenya (and Rhodesia) group had to face problems of segregation which were nonexistent for the groups in French West Africa. I stayed at a hotel just outside of Nairobi, as there was no room in the tents. I'll never forget the stony glare of the hotel receptionist, formerly as sweet as honey, when I brought Negro and white Crossroaders back to the hotel for a meal. Although most places in Nairobi were supposedly integrated, one couldn't avoid those segregated eyes.

The response of the African hotel staff to the arrival of African and American Negro guests at the hotel was delightful. On one occasion a mixed group came back from the work project to shower and change clothes before going to the American consulate for lunch. They arrived coated with the ever-present red dust. The pristine white tile of my bathroom turned into a background for what looked like creative toe painting in red clay. One glance at the glorious mess would justify the reprimands of any housekeeper. However, the African house staff kept slipping into my room with armfuls of fresh white towels and big grins of approval.

Another evening three Crossroaders came for dinner. Two were white boys and the third was a Negro girl. We were having a very gay conversation until the question came up as to how they were going to get back to the campsite, about eight miles away. The Crossroaders explained that they usually hitchhiked in and out of town in the evening. They had discovered that they had to segregate their groups in order to get a ride. Africans would pick up Negroes and white settlers would pick up white Crossroaders, but no car would stop for a mixed group. My Negro guest said to the boys, "What shall we do? I can't hitchhike alone at night, and if you stay with me you'll never get a ride."

"We can walk back," the boys said.

The girl looked down at her high heels. She was quiet for a

while, and then excused herself from dinner because she wasn't feeling well. She went back to my room and lay down. I suggested that she stay overnight with me. It was an escape but not a solution for the many cruel and unpredictable embarrassments that a Negro suffers almost daily in a segregated society. I could have easily chucked my supper too.

I was fortunate to be in Kenya the same week as the Robinsons. It was a chance to witness not only how much the Crossroaders benefited by their wisdom, but also how much they meant to the Africans. One day we drove some hundred miles northwest of Nairobi, where Doctor Robinson had been asked to speak at a mission church. It was a spectacular drive. The sky has a special look in Kenya, where thousands of little sunlit clouds form a celestial cotton field which makes the heavens appear vaster and at the same time closer. The countryside has an ever-interesting variety of landscape with hills and dales and forests and meadows, all enhancing one another. There are just enough giraffes, zebras, and baboons in unexpected places to satisfy one's preconceived notion of what Africa should look like. (The Crossroaders in French West Africa had to visit zoos to see these animals.) The consistently thatch-bonneted circular mud huts lend a harmony of shape as they cluster like giant mushrooms on the hillsides. We drove by the magnificent Rift Valley, where a few Africans are now beginning to acquire farms. Robert Frost's famous lines from "The Gift Outright" kept churning through my mind. "The land was ours before we were the land's." Who was "possessing what 'they' were unpossessed by?" Who was "possessed by what 'they' now no more possessed?" This was the riddle of Kenya.

Nakuru was a crowded township. Many Africans had been forced to move there from the Rift Valley during the Mau Mau emergency. We drove past rows and rows of little houses and stopped at Reverend John Kirobi's house next to the church. It was a good-sized church, obviously unfinished. The sun was just setting as we entered. The wind was blowing in gusts through the paneless windows. The altar consisted of a wooden table covered with a cloth which kept fluttering in the evening breeze. On the left side of the church the women were sitting, while the men occupied the benches on the right. Reverend Robinson mounted the platform with an interpreter and Reverend Kirobi. I had been wondering what was in the large bundle Reverend Kirobi was carrying, and the mystery was solved when he presented Robinson with a large, magnificent cloak made of baboon skin. This special gift was a symbol of the people's esteem and affection.

Robinson seemed to appreciate the physical as well as the spiritual warmth of this present. As he stood there in the twilight addressing the congregation, he wrapped the baboon skin snugly around. He told the people of Nakuru how he had once been starving, cold, and rejected—experiences with which they were all too familiar. He went on to say that at that very discouraging time of his life he couldn't possibly have believed that one day he would become a leader known in almost every country in the world. He pointed to the congregation and said, "Each one of you has the same opportunity. Only you have to work and study very hard for results. God has a unique place of service for each one of us." The faces of the listening people showed that they could not help gathering courage from what he had said. The American success story too often abridges its chapters on work and study, and sounds like pure luck in its overseas rendition, thereby losing its real message.

After Reverend Robinson sat down, the local chief's wife rose in the back of the church. She said she would like to have Mrs. Robinson describe to the women of Nakuru the occupations of the women in America, so that they also could take courage. Mrs. Robinson bobbed up, looking lovely as usual, a pale blue cardigan over her shoulders. She told of the jobs women hold in the United States. I thought she had forgotten "housewife," but she managed to slip that in at the end! The meeting closed with Robinson suggesting that the Crossroaders who would soon be working on a YMCA project at nearby Lake Naivasha might like to come up and have a dance with the people of Nakuru in their church. He was told that dancing was not allowed in their church. He hastily allowed that Crossroaders like to dance outside church too.

We returned to Reverend Kirobi's house for supper. This time Mrs. Robinson and I did not join the women. We sat in the front room with the men while the women crouched over black pots and white-hot charcoal burners preparing our meal in the rear of the house where they ate by themselves. Shy little boys gathered around Robinson while he sang a song about a mouse. The Africans sang for us and Robinson led everyone into singing some mighty "Alleluias."

It is a great asset for Crossroads that Robinson has such a natural relationship with so many of the African leaders. He met several, such as Nkrumah, in his student days at Lincoln University. The day after our trip to Nakuru he was flown to Maralai, where Jomo Kenyatta was still in confinement. After a four-hour conference, Kenyatta turned to Robinson and said, "We see eye to eye on many things." This does not make Robinson a Mau Mau! What it does mean is that an American has reached this great controversial figure of Kenyatta, whom the British blame for the Mau Mau uprisings, and to whom the Kenyans look as their one great hope in uniting the people for independence. A strong point can be made in favor of the thesis that, although Kenyatta was the recognized leader of the Kikuyu, he was not responsible for the Mau Mau terrorism which got out of control. It is hard to see beyond the gouged-out eyes described in our newspapers to the magnetic eyes of Jomo Kenyatta and realize that he could be the man of the moment in Kenya.

This man, educated in England, imprisoned and confined for nine years, is now free. He has the opportunity not only to unite the discordant Africans but to relate them constructively to the British.

The Crossroaders also found a chance to talk with Kenyatta.

He was released just before they left Kenya, and two of the Negro Crossroaders helped unpack china in his home in preparation for his return. The rest of the Crossroaders were determined to meet him, but so were thousands of others. The Crossroaders, never daunted by anything, wangled an interview by saying, "Robinson is your friend and he is our chief. Therefore you must see us!" Crossroaders are not easy people to turn down.

One of the most respected men in Kenya is the leader of the Kikuyu, Chief Njiiri. More than any other man, he is said to be most responsible for the final suppression of the Mau Mau rebellion, while Kenyatta was virtually helpless in prison. Chief Njiiri was awarded the Order of the British Empire for his courage. He was wounded in the fighting and his four sub-chiefs were killed. He lives about eighty miles north of Nairobi at Fort Hall, a Kikuyu township. His family consists of thirty-five wives and over a hundred children (it is considered bad luck to count).

One of his sons, Kariuki Njiiri, was in India in 1951 when he met Reverend Robinson, who encouraged and helped him to come to Lincoln University. While Kariuki Njiiri was in New York City he met Robinson's secretary, whom he married and took back to Nairobi. He is now an active member of Legco (the Legislative Council, which will form the Assembly when Kenya becomes independent) which gained an African majority in 1961.* This was all part of the background for a wonderful invitation from Chief Njiiri to the Robinsons and all eighteen Crossroaders to come up to Fort Hall for a feast.

We arrived at Fort Hall on a bus. The village was like many we had passed on our three-hour drive—a cluster of circular mud huts with thatch-helmeted roofs. We were met by Chief Njiiri, a vigorous man at ninety-two. He was dressed in a baboon-skin tunic, bedecked with medals, and a cocky beret perched over his strong face, which crinkled with merriment. His ears were arrest-

* After the release of Kenyatta, Kariuki Njiiri resigned his Legco seat to make a vacancy for the election of Kenyatta so that he could officially attend the London Constitutional Conference at Lancaster. Kariuki Njiiri is now Education and Public Relations Secretary of KANU.

ing; the lobes were pierced, stretched, and extended so that they took on more of the appearance of an open mouth than an ear. Having yanked my own ear in wonderment, I decided this must be a very painful procedure. It is done with weights. The stretched ear lobes serve as a symbol of strength as well as an object for decoration.

The Chief was followed by several wives. The older ones all had the same pierced ears with dozens of beaded earrings, the size of bracelets, decorating these unnatural appendages. Their heads were shaven so shiny smooth that I suspected this must necessitate daily attention. There is something about a shaven head that seems much more nude than an exposed breast. Maybe it's the more-naked-than-nature look that is so startling.

They were lean women, dressed inconspicuously, and all slightly stooped. The women of Kenya carry all their loads on their backs. The contrast in posture with the women of West Africa, who carry everything but their babies on their heads, is striking. The wives shuffled together about the courtyard like a chorus rather than like individuals. They reacted as one, with long "Ehs" to any of our clownish attempts at communication.

The younger wives were not shaven and their ears were like ours. Several had the babies of the ninety-two-year-old Chief on their backs.

The Chief was leading a white sheep, which baa-ed alongside him like a faithful pet. The Crossroaders gathered in the central meeting place between the huts so that the Chief could give his welcoming speech, translated from Kikuyu to English by his son, Kariuki. The Chief welcomed us with a whole-hearted expression of hospitality. He explained that the greatest honor he could pay us as a host was to slaughter his baa-ing follower in front of us and prepare it for the feast to which we had been invited. This gesture signified that we would be welcome not only that day but any day thereafter. It was a sort of eternal welcome.

The killing of the sheep was gory. His neck was slashed between baa-ings. The intestines were soon laid out on the ground for all to see. A large fire prepared for the roasting was the center of interest for several hours. Although Crossroader faces were screwed up in protest, cameras were clicking frantically to catch every stage of the dismemberment of the beast. I couldn't help thinking of the future after-dinner Crossroad audiences who would be seeing slide after slide of a sheep's guts instead of the enchanting villages and sweeping views we had driven past too quickly and jouncily to photograph on our way.

When the sheep was finally roasted it really was delicious. We were asked to make ourselves at home and eat with our fingers. A hollowed gourd filled with palm wine and a sheep's horn filled with home-made beer were passed around like loving cups. There were other Kikuyu recipes in attractive gourd serving dishes.

After the feast the wives of the Chief joined together to sing a "Happy Song," accompanied by a rhythmic dipping of the knees and a beckoning motion of the arms. The refrain reminded me of sounds I had heard only in the Canadian woods: the shrill cry of a wild loon, followed by the grunting noise expressed by a bull moose. The Crossroaders joined in this dance. It was a "natural" for them, and the wives accepted their participation with great hilarity. The fun continued when the wives surrounded the American daughter-in-law, Ruth Njiiri, and acted out the ceremony of shaving her head, crying out, "We want you to be one of us."

We were consumed with curiosity to peer into one of the mysterious little huts. When we were finally invited, it was a great disappointment, for it was so dark that we couldn't even discern a shapely shadow. We did visit the Chief's house, which was set apart from the mud huts. It was a rectangular white-washed structure like any other house with doors and windows and simple furniture. There were pictures hung around the ceiling, among which the Chief proudly pointed out one taken of himself and Robinson in 1954.

One of the really impressive things about this red-letter day was the graceful dignity with which the two cultures of the different generations of Njiiris met. It would be hard to imagine a greater contrast between the customs of father and son. Yet with all these differences there was mutual respect. Kariuki introduced his parents with great pride, saying, "This is my real home." The old Chief, who had no desire to conform to the modern world, was bursting with pride over his up-and-coming son, so active in the life of Nairobi today.

This was not an unusual family situation for any part of Africa. Everywhere leaders and the people who may become leaders are facing the kind of political and economic changes in one generation that our civilization has accomplished in five or six, and they are confronted with cultural changes that we have never had to face even gradually. To bridge such wide cultural gaps without losing track of the human touchstones between two generations is a real art. It is essential for the development of Africa that these touchstones be guarded.

That rare day in the heart of Africa emphasized the privilege of being associated with Crossroads. The Crossroaders were in an ideal situation. They were unhampered by the strict, inhibiting responsibilities of a government job, and yet they had just enough of a job to be thoroughly involved. The usefulness of students in our foreign policy has been questioned by some people. What can these young people do? They have the vitality, curiosity, and freedom to experience informal, down-to-earth relationships with many different people that others with an official capacity cannot.

The next day provided the perfect contrast in the type of experience one runs into as a tourist. I ordered a car to go to the Nairobi National Game Park, and invited several Crossroaders to fill it up. I was told that the driver really knew where the lions were. I was glad of this opportunity to check lions off my list, as I hadn't had time to see many of the other tourist "musts," such as Victoria Falls, Kariba Dam, and Mount Kilimanjaro. The park was divided into sections, and scouts radioed back to the main gate information as to where the lions were lying. At six o'clock each evening the animals would arise and prowl. The whole day was planned around being at the right place at the right time. We were told at the entrance gate that section seven was where the lions were that afternoon, and we still had time to drive around and observe many other interesting animals before attending the main feature. There were whole families of humorous baboons. (I wondered whether the two coats I had seen in the past week were in any way related.) They romped all over our taxi, and we had to shut the windows so they wouldn't climb in. We would count them by their shadows as they rode along on the trunk rack. They somersaulted off the back of the car as we drove on.

In my lessons on lion lore I had learned that one clue to their whereabouts is the absence of other animals. We came to a place where there wasn't a zebra in sight—a sure sign that the king of beasts must be crouching nearby. Even the Crossroaders were giving me the lion line. We saw a Mercedes-Benz parked on the far side of a dell which we were approaching, and our driver whispered in excitement that this was just the place. We drove carefully up to the dell and parked across from the Mercedes-Benz. Then we waited, alert and eager for just a twitch of grass to suggest the location of the lion. We waited for about a half hour in taut anticipation. The driver reassured us that there must be a lion or the Mercedes wouldn't be parked there for such a long time. Our time was running out and I, who find even an ostrich exciting, thought we might be overdoing this lion-waiting. I suggested to the driver that we drive around the dell, park next to the Mercedes, and share its superior view of the lion. He thought enough of this tourist suggestion to act on it. We drove around the mystery place and chugged up alongside the Mercedes hopefully. In it was a couple in fond embrace. Our driver, undaunted, leaned out the window and asked eagerly, "You see lions?" The boy unwrapped his arms from around his prey and answered sheepishly, "No, no lions here." Later we finally did find some lions, along with about sixty other much less romantic cars.

6

Contrasts

EVEN MORE INTERESTING THAN THE INITIAL CULTURAL SHOCK, EX-
perienced by contrasting wherever one comes from outside Africa with whatever one first meets up with inside Africa, are the
many contrasts which exist within the continent itself. Flying
from the clear, crisp, cool climate of Kenya to warm, muggy,
mosquito-ey West Africa is enervating, but counteracting the
physical letdown is the spiritual uplift from the change in racial
atmosphere. No longer does one feel the predictable gusts of hostility between black and white people, for in West Africa they
are quite naturally sharing life together. Although the countries
here have never experienced racial tensions comparable to those in
such countries as Kenya and the Rhodesias, their recently acquired
independence gives them the added dignity of being in control.
The difference between visiting Africans in Kenya and Nigeria is
comparable to the difference between visiting a friend in a hotel or
in his home. There is no question in West Africa that one is calling on the African "at home."

All Crossroaders shared a definite ideal as to what the Crossroads work project should accomplish. With seventeen groups in a

continent of contrasts, it was understandable that the different groups would have some contrasting experiences. Not every group could realize all the aspects of the preconceived ideal of a work project. The ideal was best realized by adding the sum total of the separate Crossroads experiences.

Although the work project was considered a means and not an end in itself, it was still important that it be well chosen, to fill an imminent community need. This was not always easy. The Africans submitted requests for what they considered to be desirable projects, and they didn't always understand the Crossroads purpose. The Chief at Nkwatia in Ghana was so pleased with the schoolhouse the Crossroaders built for St. Peter's College that he invited them to return the following year to build him a palace. It took a lot of explaining to make clear that schools have priority over palaces for Crossroads projects!

The planning of a project was usually done through the Department of Youth and Sports, Social Welfare, and Education, or whoever seemed to be the most appropriate agent in the desired community. Two members of the Crossroads staff would go to Africa during the winter to make arrangements for the summer. Sometimes those plans were canceled out by a change of personnel in the local government. Most of the unsatisfactory aspects of the work projects could be traced to insufficient planning, and the Crossroads staff realized that this was the most important field to concentrate on in order to insure the success of future projects. What was really needed was a permanent Crossroads office in West Africa and one in East Africa. This is a hope for the future; at present there are not sufficient funds.

Every Crossroader wanted to see the concrete results of his labors. It was important for their morale that the project be one that could be finished during the summer, but this was very hard to plan with so many unknown factors. When the Africans planned a project, for example, they had no idea how much work to expect from the Americans. The classic example of underestimation was the Kenya project, described in the last chapter, where what had been estimated to take a month was accomplished in three days. Other groups had projects which never even reached the halfway mark by the end of the summer.

It was not the intention of the Crossroaders to work alone. Ideally, the project was a joint endeavor with all the people of the community. The Africans might just watch for several days, but then they pitched in. Along with community participation, it was the Crossroads plan to have an African student group working with them on each project. This was more difficult to arrange. School calendars were different and classes were often in session. Students who boarded wanted to go home for their vacations, and many had to get paying jobs to support their education. The biggest obstacle of all was the illusion that a person, once educated, need never soil his hands again. The Crossroads group in Sierra Leone had an ideal setup, working with a group of students from Fourah Bay College, while some of the other groups had to scavenge for students.

In Nigeria there was one project which came close to fulfilling the Crossroads ideal of what a work project should be, and another that came close to illustrating exactly what a Crossroads work project should not be. The work projects at Achina and Lagos make interesting comparisons.

Achina was in the eastern section of Nigeria, where two other Crossroads groups had worked previously. The African students who worked with them had talked a lot about Crossroads, and this year's group benefited from the publicity. It had been a government policy to take an active part in community development. The Office of Community Development played an important role in stimulating the villagers to work on their own projects. This tradition of activity in community development was a perfect background for a Crossroads project. The director, Mr. Ndu, not only gave the Crossroaders every help in the work project, but arranged for week-end trips from there throughout the region. The government gave eleven Nigerian students a stipend of about half of what they would have earned during the summer, making it possible for them to live and work with the fourteen Crossroaders the entire time they were in Achina.

Achina was a village built high on a hill with a lovely view of the surrounding valley. The greatest inconvenience of this village was the location of the well at the bottom of a very steep bank overgrown with the rotting roots of trees. The women, with their babes on back and pails on head, had a precarious journey groping their slippery, uncertain way down the bank and scrambling back without spilling their precious loads of water. The Crossroad project was to build cement steps from the top of the town to the well. Clearing the overgrowth for a path was a job in itself. The four hundred villagers who joined in the project were astounded to see white men working with them and not simply directing them. They beat out messages on their talking drums, calling the people across the valley to come and help in the work.

After the path was cleared, the Crossroaders and the Africans built the wood forms for the steps, made their own gravel, and mixed their own cement. There was great satisfaction in pouring the cement into the forms and being able to count their daily progress in the number of steps completed. Each step bore the name of a Nigerian or American worker. It would take 286 steps from top to bottom. When 186 steps had been completed, the Crossroaders had to leave Achina for a few days to work on a soil-erosion project. When they returned, they were greeted with a most gratifying surprise. The villagers, who had been taught how to use the cement mixer themselves, had carried on with their own voluntary labor and finished the 286 steps. To stimulate people to help themselves is one of the big aims of the work project. Few Crossroaders had the satisfaction of seeing their works of labor not only finished but put to use before they left. The stately procession of water carriers gracefully descending the stairs to the well was a real contrast to the scramble they had witnessed on arrival. Also rewarding was the news that after the Crossroaders left Achina the villagers initiated a similar project of making more steps down to another lower spring.

Although the project in Lagos did not have the ready-made elements of a good Crossroads work project, many a Crossroader remarked, "We learn most when things go wrong." The Crossroaders had a lot to teach me.

The Lagos group were living in Queen's College overlooking the race tracks, and their spacious quarters were isolated from the kind of contacts they were seeking with Africans. However, no other group had a grandstand view of the local horse races from their bedroom balconies! Their work project was one of street cleaning in one of the poorest sections of Lagos. The plan was for them to work from four to seven P.M. each day so that some of the local people could help with the project when they got home from work. This left the Crossroaders unoccupied until four P.M. There were interesting things to see in Lagos, but no one was in the mood for daily sightseeing. It was a real challenge for the individual Crossroaders to find work to fill in this time. One girl, who was a nurse, volunteered at a Lagos Hospital. Others found useful things to do, but it was a hit-or-miss arrangement, and they wasted precious time in the process.

When I visited the late-afternoon street-cleaning work project, it seemed to me like the worst possible Crossroads plan. While I stood in the warm drizzle amid masses of exuberant Africans, watching the Crossroaders digging out the ditches to alleviate the drainage of the open sewers, trying to recall the names of all those deadly diseases they might be catching, all the Crossroads ideals seemed out of sight and futile.

One of the town leaders, mistakenly assuming that I had some sort of authority, led me down to the jungly section at the foot of the street, where the drainage had choked, and explained that he would like the Crossroaders to relieve this bit of swampy overgrowth so that the sewage could pass on farther from the town before it came to a standstill. I wanted to wrap up each Crossroader in cellophane and send him or her straight back to the United States. Someone whispered to me that no cement was forthcoming and that the first good downpour would probably wash out the yards and yards of carefully dug ditches. The people of the town were swarming around the Crossroaders in such a state of curiosity that there was hardly any room through which to push the mud-laden wheelbarrows. Some Africans had joined in the work too, but there were more looking on. How could anyone relate to this city mob? But as I watched the Crossroaders cheerfully sloshing in the sewers I realized that no one shared my depression. They were intent on doing whatever job they had been asked to do.

As I was standing there, dazed and discouraged on the dismal street, I felt a tap on my arm. A voice from the crowd was quietly saying, "Mainland one seventeen." The voice repeated it several times before I really heard it. "Mainland one seventeen." Why did it sound so familiar? Suddenly it dawned on me that, of course, I was staying at the Mainland Hotel in Lagos and my room number was one seventeen. I looked around to see the familiar face of the boy who took care of my room. I asked him where he lived and he quickly invited me back to his home. We walked down a side street, turned right and left through several narrow alleys, and entered one of the whitewashed mud houses. He led me down a little corridor to his room. It was whitewashed and square, with a small window opposite the door. The sleeping section was curtained off at one side. The remaining wall was used like a bulletin board. Jesus Christ shared honors with Queen Elizabeth, some defiant boxers, and delicious bathing beauties.

There were two chairs and a table, and I was invited to sit down. A series of relatives poked their heads in the door for quick, grinning introductions. My host excused himself for a minute and came back with a quart of ice-cold German beer. I thought of course he was going to share this generous portion with me, but he explained that he was in training to be a boxer. He wanted to see the world and meet the people outside Nigeria. He had decided that the intellectual competition for scholarships was too stiff and that his best bet was in the field of athletics. (I was glad to be able to whip out snapshots of our two wrestling sons.) Although I had followed the Olympic games, I had not realized the great possibilities for international communication through sports. (A sociologist from South Africa, who visited us over Christmas, is convinced that athletics may be the best wedge to pry open that closed door of South Africa to the rest of the world.) As I looked up at the faces on the "bulletin board" I had a fresh feeling of wonder at the variety of different gifts endowed in human beings for the purpose of communication. This boy's one chance to experience the world outside Nigeria was his ability to "knock the other fellow out."

I was having such a nice visit with my friend from the Main-land Hotel that I nearly missed my ride back with the Crossroaders. There were hundreds of Africans surrounding our bus, all asking for addresses so that they might correspond with "someone" in the United States. After all, if Americans were either crazy enough or angelic enough to help clean out their sewers, there was no end to what one could expect of them. The pressure of the excited Africans around us made me feel uneasy, like a goal post after a football game, and at the mercy of the emotions of the crowd. The Crossroaders seemed completely at ease. One young man persisted in asking for my address. I didn't have the heart to say no. I was a coward without the courage to be either honest or totally dishonest. I refused to give my own name, so, in my confusion, I fumbled out the name and address of my mother, assuming he would never get it straight.

After disentangling myself from several other approachers, I noticed John Hubbell, the Crossroads area leader, giving a sort of speech to about forty surrounding Africans who had all pleaded for his address. He was explaining very carefully that, although he could come and work in their town, he had a job as a teacher at home and would never have time to get to his students if he stopped to correspond with every African acquaintance; he could write to a few special friends, but not to hundreds! They listened. It made sense. They seemed to understand. I realized then how very important it is for genial Americans, whose good will appears to have no boundaries, to make clear their limitations, thereby avoiding obligations they can't possibly live up to.

That day when I had come closest to rejecting the whole idea of Crossroads was perhaps the day that brought home to me most clearly the fact that there is no situation too little or too big for communication between human beings, and that every contact is charged with either plus or minus. This is the overwhelming, ever-present challenge for all Americans in Africa. It is a challenge which Crossroaders seem quite naturally aware of.

When I returned to the United States, one of the first things my mother said to me was, "Oh, I got the nicest letter from one of your African friends." At first I couldn't think who in Africa could have possibly written my mother. She added, "It was mailed from Lagos," and I blushed—with humiliation.

7

Togo—

Life in Bushtown

As you fly over the Dahomey-Togo coastline, the fringed palms, sandy shore, and ever-pounding surf stretch out in parallels as far as you can see between the brownish-green land and bluish-green ocean. It is easy on the eyes.

We flew very low over Dahomey, and I stayed glued to the porthole in my eagerness to spot the location of the school which our son David had helped to build with the Crossroads group the preceding summer. The shore was dotted with possible Crossroads cement creations. There were also dugout canoes drawn up next to the airy grass fishing shacks. David had described going out with his fishermen friends at four A.M., breaking through the surf and paddling like mad past the rollers on to the calmer waters. Just a year before, Dahomey had gained its independence, and to celebrate the great day David and other Crossroaders had led some thousand Africans in a conga line through the streets of Grand Popo. They made two round trips dancing from one end of the town to the other. "We could have gotten elected to any office that day," he wrote home.

After flying past Grand Popo, we knew we must be over Togo. We soon landed in Lomé, its capital city. The new Lomé airport had just opened and was like a Walt Disney creation in its toylike charm—this littlest airport for this littlest sliver of a country "behind-the-sea" (the translation of the Ewe word "Togo"). As soon as the engines quieted and the doors were opened we could hear music. A chorus of lovely girls dressed in white was on the observation deck singing as only the Togolese can sing. They were schoolgirls gathered to greet their president, Sylvanus Olympio, who was expected on the next plane. This glamorous introduction to Togo gave little indication of the great poverty of the land.

Inside the airport, as spectacular as any advertisement, were pictures of Crossroaders together with Togolese *Voluntaires au Travail* building a schoolhouse. The captions were good and the Crossroaders looked quite at home in Togoland. I could hardly wait to join them. They were living about sixty miles to the north in the village of Womé, and there was a train that chugged right through the bush from Lomé to a town near Womé called Palimé.

Although the train was like a market place on wheels, it could still put the New York-New Haven to shame for cleanliness. It stopped at several little "stations" where women and children were waiting to trot alongside the tracks selling their ground nuts, cassava, coconuts, and maize. The cloths they had wrapped around them were colorful reminders of Togo's recently acquired independence, for on them was printed in gay designs "27 *Avril* 1960."

When I got off the train at Palimé I looked around for a lorry that might take me to Womé. The lorry is a kind of truck commonly known as a "mammy wagon." Curiously enough, they are owned by the women, and they are *the* vehicles of transportation in Africa. People and more people are packed in with their livestock and deadstock about double capacity. The overloading doesn't impede the speed one single bit. With the spirit of an elephant chase the Africans make sport of driving their mammy wagons. They are not bound by any definite route or scheduled stops. Their destination is determined by the passengers, and the passengers are picked up as they appear on the road. Every mammy wagon has a motto, such as "Fear Women" and "The Sea Never Runs Dry." One really needs a motto before boarding a mammy wagon. "The Lord Delivers" proved an appropriate one for me, for I eventually arrived safely at my destination.

Womé, in Ewe, means "in the good." The Crossroaders really were "in the good," because it was the answer to every Crossroader's dream to live in such a bush town *comme les Africains*. This was the primeval forest, and the Crossroaders were taking a turn at being primeval too. Many of the other Crossroads groups working in the cities never had this chance to "try out their hardy sides," as one Crossroader put it.

The Crossroad home was a three-room schoolhouse on the edge of the village of Womé. Before I had a chance to look around, I was whisked into one of the classrooms-turned-living-dining-rooms for the immediate business of the moment. In Africa welcoming is more than an attitude vaguely expressed; it is a ritual. When the Crossroaders first arrived in the village, an elaborate series of events was staged which lasted several days. For my arrival the "welcoming" process was merely a token, but at the same time touching. The Crossroaders had fallen right into the African custom so naturally that one would think they'd spent their lives staging "welcomings." Africans and Crossroaders sat around in a circle and, to the beat of two drums, sang several Ewe songs in my honor.

The drums were often at work in this circle of Africans and Americans, for all the Crossroaders were taking "drum lessons." The Africans were tireless in their supervision of this magic beat. You could see that the Crossroaders were getting better and better at it. However, there is something enchanted about an African and his drum. The African and his drum beat together like two musical instruments, and together they can produce the effect of an orchestra. I have never heard a drum express for an American what it can for an African.

In the rear of the same classroom was a long table where the Africans and Crossroaders ate together. The African diet lacked both vitamins and variety. One could expect the same old rice or macaroni dishes with the same old *fu-fu* sauces, meal after meal. This was no small adjustment for the Crossroaders when visions of hamburgers danced in their heads after a hard working day. It was not that they couldn't have imported better food; the Crossroaders had made the decision to live just as the Africans were living, so that they might become an integral part of the Womé community life. However, they did insist on boiled and filtered drinking water. The food budget was divided between the Africans and Americans living together. To import food would have been either too expensive for the Africans or exclusive of the Americans. For the Crossroaders this was a first-hand introduction to hunger, more real than reading. As one Crossroader said, "It makes you feel different about buying a package of cigarettes when you realize that the same money would represent a day's food for an entire African family." When another Crossroader asked a small African boy the price of a loaf of bread, the child couldn't answer because he'd never had any bread in all his life. The hungry children would cluster around the windows at meal times, peering in but never begging. There was no garbage problem; the children would ravenously eat any leftovers. Fortunately there was extra food. Although the Crossroaders were missing their proteins, they were not starved for quantity of food. Several confessed that they had always taken American vitality for granted and had been quite critical of the lazier working habits of the Africans. "We'll never again criticize the inertia that comes from hunger and disease," they said. They were amazed to discover how dependent even American energy is on good health and a well-balanced diet.

This was not an experience shared by all the Crossroad groups. Most ate well. You couldn't help admiring those young people who had the discipline to put an ideal before their personal needs. Their ideal was unquestionably realized; their acceptance in the village of Womé was absolutely whole-hearted.

There was another question in my mind. I could live *comme les Africains* for a few days, and the Crossroaders for seven weeks with no real ill effects; but two years? We were all wondering about how the Peace Corps was going to make out. One could exist, but there was a risk that the enthusiasm, which got us to Africa in the first place, might gradually drain away. And what use would we be then? Our pioneering youth is too valuable to be unnecessarily de-energized. The world needs the creativity which comes from well-being. Crossroaders are very realistic pilots for our American ideals.

The last sound I would have expected to awaken me after my first night in the African bush was the ringing of church bells. As I stretched and peered through the mosquito netting, I could just read the last lesson left on the blackboard above my cot. It was hard to tell, in the row of white-gauzed cots, how many of the others were awake at five-thirty A.M. One of the African girls was rising. Her clothes were hanging in the community closet formed by the stacking of desks at the end of the classroom-turned girls' bedroom. She wrapped her sprightly blue and yellow cloth around her so that the dashing design delineated her full figure attractively. African women are very feminine and graceful. The Togolese have a Polynesian type of beauty. The girl slipped into her two-prong yellow plastic sandals—which must be high on the Japanese export market, as they were almost uniform in French West Africa. She tiptoed out of the room and left the door ajar so that I could just see the entrance to the Evangelical Mission Church across the courtyard.

An African boy was already sweeping the courtyard carefully with his short-handled twig stick. The villagers were drifting into church one by one, men, women, and children, all with their gay cloths wrapped snug in the early mistiness of the morning. The church bell continued "clang-clang-clang" until it was replaced by the strains of an organ. It's seldom one can fall right out of bed into a church service. I didn't even stop to wash. There were about fifty people standing to sing an Ewe hymn when I entered. A very earnest little minister gave a fifteen-minute sermon on what he later explained to me was "salvation." There was a constant chorus of coughs from the congregation. Was this early morning sinus or T.B.? Who would know in this country, where the ratio of doctors to population is one to forty thousand?

Although the Africans have many disadvantages in life, I couldn't help thinking they get off to a privileged start. African babies have a wonderful existence. There they were in church, slung around their mothers' warm backs, still nodding in limp contentment, the crucial source of life hanging large and available just around the corner. African babies don't suffer from boredom or loneliness. In the sunny market place their fuzzy little heads peek around the curves of their mothers to see what's new and interesting. In the dim kerosene light they are jounced to the beat of the drum as their mothers take a fling at dancing the high life. No wonder the smallest African child is as musical as a quarter note. The baby's desirable position is not altered when his mother takes additional loads on her head. He is not left behind when she goes to the river for water. But the African child does well if he can hold onto this initial security of his first year or two, for there is nothing gradual about his displacement when the next child is born. He relinquishes the maternal breast and back simultaneously and moves right on to an adult diet on his own two little feet, catching what free rides he can on the backs of his older brothers and sisters. The infant mortality is high at this transitional stage when the child is separated from his mother. Most African women can count as many dead as living children in their families.

For all ages of African children, the Crossroaders are natural Pied Pipers. Hordes of children followed them in their every activity all day long. It started with the early morning trips to the river. Much of life centered around the fetching of water, of which the river, about three quarters of a mile from the village, was the only source. Every bucket of water used for drinking, cooking, or washing represented somebody's one-and-a-half-mile walk. There was a large tank beside the schoolhouse that held about one hundred bucketfuls. The walk to the river was through the forest of gigantic trees, which rose above the lush verdure like a Gothic cathedral. The cotton tree seemed king of them all; its mammoth roots were like buttresses with partitions as large as closets. Palm trees were everywhere; and you could pick coffee and cocoa beans alongside the path. The trip was a very social one, with a constant exchange of greetings. "*Oon-di-lo?*" was a safe, all-inclusive Ewe phrase. It meant, "How are you, your household, and your children?" all at once. The Crossroaders would swing their buckets jauntily as they approached the river, but returning was the real balance test. They would hold their hands high in uneasy support of the pails precariously balanced on their heads, while the water sloshed in little dribbles over their faces. The less expert, like myself, would keep shifting the pail from one dragging arm to the other. There was no question as to which was the tireless method of carriage, but we weren't all blessed with a water carrier's equilibrium. Africans carried their gourds or pails, full of water, with the grace and ease of a new Easter bonnet.

It is *de rigueur* in Womé for a newcomer to call on the village Chief and the village Queen within twenty-four hours of arrival. The village Queen is unrelated to the Chief; while he inherits his position, she is elected as the most respected woman in the community. The women discuss their problems with the Queen in the same manner that the men confer with the Chief. The daily rain had just ceased when we started out to pay our respects to the Chief, the Queen, and the various town elders. The muddy rivulets made it very slippery underfoot. The raft of children who had become an integral part of the Crossroads family were eager to show the *bienvenue* their village. Leading the way, they sketched little dance steps in the mud with their restless toes. Their graceful motions suggested the smaller creatures of the forest. They were quick to point out anything of interest: the men weaving baskets and drying out coffee beans, the frisky miniature black goats, and the trees from which they made their *ekpuis*. The ekpui is a favorite musical instrument consisting of two balls attached by a string. The player would hold one ball in the palm of his hand and flip the other around from side to side, making a rhythmical click like a castanet. The children were as adept with their slingshots as with their ekpuis: their two most treasured possessions. These friendly children were very alert, and the Crossroaders who had taken on tutorial jobs found them most rewarding pupils. Most of these children would go to the Primary School in Womé, but there was slim chance for further education, as there were only two or three secondary schools in Togo.

The children took us to the community kitchen where the village wives assembled to prepare meals for the Crossroaders. The women were crouched on small stools over steaming black pots. The smoke from the twig fires was very tear-provoking, and I felt like a sissy until I noticed the African women were having the same difficulty.

Outside the community kitchen women were pounding manioc in large wooden pestles. Manioc is a plant with tuberous roots, about three times the size of a sweet potato, which is the staple of the local diet. They boil them and fry them and mash them. *Fu-fu* is made by pounding the manioc into a white pulp. After about fifteen minutes of pounding and a sprinkle of water, the substance becomes rubbery and shiny like a ball. It is pure starch and rather tasteless. The Africans serve it with very peppery sauces. The Crossroaders soon learned that you are not supposed to chew it, but swallow it—"like medicine," as one of them said.

After visiting the community kitchen we stopped at the home of one of the elders, whose duty it was to take us to call on the Chief. (The Queen was not at home.) He was also to act as an interpreter, for the Chief spoke only Ewe. The Chief had already been alerted that there was a foreigner in the village. It was fortunate for me that Mia Choumenkovitch, the Crossroads leader, could tell me how to behave, for one must follow tradition while calling on a Chief. We were led into his hut and asked to sit down on the assembled chairs. In a few minutes the Chief entered. He was about seventy years old. His colorful *pagne* was similar to those worn by the other elders of the village. It was not the robe but the way he wore it that distinguished him as Chief; there was a slight but significant difference in the way his pagne was draped over his bare dark shoulder and in the manner with which his hands gathered up the folds. After he sat down, we rose to shake hands with him and returned to our seats. The Chief must be the first to speak. The conversation is traditional. He inquired as to the health and welfare of every branch of my family. I assured him that everyone was flourishing. We then exchanged the usual pleasantries about how glad he was and how fortunate I was to be in Womé. He sent for a bottle of orange pop, which is considered a great delicacy. It was customary for the visitor to bring a small present. Then it was my turn to inquire about the welfare of the community. It was traditional for the Chief to remain seated when we arose to shake hands and say our farewells.

The Chief was proud of his village and the community life that made it possible. He had explained how he gave each villager a parcel of land along with the permission to build on it. When anyone built a house in Womé, everyone joined in pounding and molding the wet mud bricks. Then there was a waiting period of six months before the bricks were sufficiently dry to assemble into a house. The final thatching of the roof was another community project. These houses were rectangular, with windows, a variation in mud architecture from the predominantly circular type in Kenya.

Most of the men were farmers. When one man's manioc field was ready for weeding, the others would join together and help him with the task. This spirit was typical of every side of tribal life. The Ewe tribe was spread out in such a way that when the colonial powers created the countries of Ghana, Togo, and Dahomey the Ewes suffered a three-way split. Womé was very close to the Ghanian border. What had once been forest and fields between cousins was now sealed off with gates and guards. Crossing the border necessitated showing a pass, changing from the right to the left side of the road, using different currency, speaking another tongue, and breathing a very different political atmosphere. It was cramping for casual communication and disastrous for cooperative living. Typical of the obstacles created by these borders between countries was the sending of a telegram. Although its destination might be only a few miles away, it had to be routed from Togo to Paris to London and back to Ghana again. The talking drums were far simpler!

The enthusiastic participation of the Crossroaders in the Togolese community projects gave fresh encouragement to a spirit which had been thwarted for many years. The Voluntaires au Travail with whom the Crossroaders were working was a private Togolese agency recently started by a few young men who wanted to re-stimulate this spirit of self-help in this newly independent country. They were conducting seven work camps in different parts of the country.

Womé had requested a new primary school building and twenty Togolese students, as members of the Voluntaires au Travail, had given up the time working on their own farms and paid their own lorry fares to come and help build it. The people of Womé paid for the materials, supplied food for the visiting workers, and also participated in the work project. Every night the town crier would go from house to house calling out the names of the people who were asked to report at the work project the next day. The schoolhouse was planned by the community on a very large scale: two hundred feet by fifty feet with two stories. Although there was great need for such a schoolhouse, it was much too ambitious a project for the Crossroaders and their African co-workers to think of finishing in one summer. The absence of a port in Togo increased the difficulties of obtaining the necessary building materials. The available supplies were quite inadequate.

The Crossroaders spent many days transporting rocks by head from a nearby mountain to fill in the foundations for the school. It was a lovely walk up the mountain, and you could hear the African and American workers singing and talking all the way. This was the kind of bond that made it possible for the students to talk very frankly about the idiosyncrasies of their respective countries. However, it was hard on morale that the work project turned out to be more of a "means" than an "end" in itself. No matter how gratifying it was to get to know the Africans, the Crossroaders wanted desperately to make real progress on the school. Its completion seemed like a pretty remote dream. One of the hardest adjustments for Americans working in Africa is that of repressing our great desire for organization, efficiency, and expediency, and mustering up the patience to stay sane at a slackened pace. The Crossroaders knew that the work project was their *raison d'être* in Womé; but life in Womé was very rewarding.

The evenings were always gay in Womé. For almost all Crossroads groups the high-life dances were among the happy memories of the summer. As one Crossroader said, "High life is one big smile!" The Crossroad girls would usually wear their African dresses to these affairs. Sometimes they would lend their American dresses to the African girls. All ages participated, the oldest and youngest syncopating with equal abandon around the dance floor. Dancing is a first language for the Africans; with it they express everything best. The ecstasy of their dance is irresistible, and it is their great desire to include everyone in sharing this joy. Although their living conditions seem depressing to us, the Africans exude happiness with a contagion that makes material comfort seem utterly unimportant.

The Crossroaders also had their musical contributions to make. Stu Rawlings' guitar was a great addition to many occasions. He had a nice variety of American songs to sing, and the Africans loved it. A musical instrument is one of the most valuable assets anyone could have when traveling in Africa, for music reaches out so much faster than words. Stu described how he and his guitar participated in the life of the village: "The night that Godwin Doghe died we arrived at his home at nine o'clock. About two hundred people sat with us in the courtyard, weeping as they sang hymns along with a small organ. I was asked to play a song on my guitar, and this I did with the background of majestic palms silhouetted by a full moon."

There is drama to everyday life in the bush, but the Africans also create drama out of it. Africans love to act in plays, and Crossroaders always have a creative comeback. The stage provided the opportunity for some of the best cultural exchanges between Africans and Crossroaders.

The Ewes specialize in cantats, which are morality plays repeated to music. Most themes are taken from the Bible, but one of the summer hits was entitled, "Had I Only Known." Through six hours of rhythm, color, swords, dancers, and a cast of dozens, a young girl learns to obey her mother. The large audiences are as expressive as the actors, often inserting their own dialogues into the proceedings.

The Crossroaders staged a return cantat—"Little Red Riding Hood" turned into an allegory about Togo. Sylvanus Olympio, the President and leader of Togo independence, became the woodsman. Little Red Riding Hood was the New Togo, and the grandmother, traditional Togo. And the wolf? France, of course. This was not a play the Crossroaders wanted reviewed in Paris.

Although the Crossroaders had come to Africa to learn about Africans, they were also learning a lot about one another, which included learning about themselves. They were discovering the real human beings so often hidden by the many differences of their varied American backgrounds. Many of them would not have been close friends in the States. Many of us tend to associate with people most like ourselves and miss the opportunity to face what is put into focus by the differences between people. There are so many easy escapes from facing oneself in the bustle of American life. Here there was no escape. This diverse group of Crossroaders was thrown together, and they were all extremely dependent on one another. One Crossroader told me, "You have no idea how much each one of us has changed this summer." It was a very maturing experience. After Mrs. Poullada, the wife of the American ambassador, visited the Crossroaders she said, "Oh, wouldn't you just love that chance to grow up in two months." There was more truth than exaggeration in what she said.

In their daily living the Crossroaders had a very intimate and total exposure to one another. Although this primitive living was exhilarating, it was also at times depressing. The toilet facilities consisted of a bamboo enclosure surrounding a deep pit transversed by logs, placed not quite so far apart as railroad ties. Straddling was a delicate art. *Comme les animaux* was preferable to *comme les Africains* in this detail. When the Crossroaders first arrived in Womé the enclosure was integrated—for the sexes. The Crossroaders felt they must compromise with the African theme at this point, and they hastily hung a bamboo curtain as a partition between the girls' and boys' rooms. It was still awkward enough in times of health. In times of diarrhea the only medicine that could save the day was a sense of humor.

The "shower" was another bamboo enclosure, but with a rock floor. The Crossroaders would line up with their buckets of water in the heat of the midday sun, dripping from the morning's labor on the work project. It was no time to dream of plunging into cool ocean surf, for that was sixty miles away. Showers from Heaven were helpful for shampoos—if they didn't cease before you had the soap rinsed out. Everyone admired the personal appearances of the Africans in this muggy climate. It would have been all too easy to forego that mile-and-a-half walk to the river as a prerequisite to cleanliness.

In this primitive life stripped of material comforts, Crossroaders grew to respect and like each other in times of ecstasy and in times of depression. They cared for one another when sick, amused one another when bored, and encouraged one another when downhearted. They were united in working together for something much bigger than themselves. Although I hesitate to mention it as an incidental value of the Crossroads experience, there have been worse preparations for marriage.

The Crossroaders did not entertain any altruistic pretenses when they went to live in Womé. They did not go to impose their values on another culture. They went to these people in the bush with the singular desire to identify with their way of life and by so doing become their friends. If they had more pretentious motives the people of Womé would not have opened wide the gates of their community life, for they were as sensitive as little children in their detection of sincerity.

The Crossroaders knew they were taking away something from Womé that they could never repay. Whereas many of the values we treasure most in the United States have become so materially overdressed that their natural form is no longer discernible, these qualities appear in their nakedness in a bushtown such as Womé. None of the Crossroaders had ever experienced such an adventure in self-reliance. There was literally nothing unless they made it so. From the Africans they learned some of the thinglessness of pure joy which can come only from within.

In all vital relationships, it is almost impossible either to give or receive a great deal without reciprocation. The Africans also had strong feelings about the Crossroaders. I quote from a letter written by one of the African Voluntaires au Travail to the Crossroaders:

Dear brother Americans,

I don't cease to think after you. Are you well? Everybody well I think.

I propose to descend at Womé on the 4 or 5 Aug. to see you before your leaving day from Togoland to wish you farewell.

From my birth day and to now I don't live between Americans and Europeans as you and from you I have got many things or characters which I don't never and never forget. For your facts are not to be forgotten. I shall not also forget anybody among you such as my professor Miss Barbara, as my melody man Mr. Stuart, as my future lawyer Mr. Thom, as my mate Mr. Bernard, as my future doctor Mr. Roger, as my quiet Miss Jeane, as my mate at kitchen Ellen, as my darling Shirley, and as my headmaster at all french and english Miss Mia. I leave you and hope to meet again after few days, send to everybody my morning kiss.

Your brother,
Godfried

When the Crossroaders were ready to leave they received a tribute from the people of Womé which could not have been bought by any amount of foreign aid or invited by any number of well-meaning speeches. Tom Gilhool describes the parting:

When Womé said good-by, they said it at a fete. The fields were idle. The village square was cleared, then filled with 1700 people. The square was closed and lorries rerouted in some tortuous way around the village. At eight in the morning the villagers began to dress Crossroaders. Pagnes, like togas, of heavy black or intricate blue. And sandals. The Crossroads leader was dressed in full honors as Queen, in gold and white, and the girls in prints and beads. The Queen's stool was carried before her with the mitre of gold and bolts of cloth. Mia had been asked to take over the position of Village Queen from 7:00 A.M. to 4:00 P.M. that day. This was a most unusual honor, particularly for a white woman. It was a serious occasion. Mia laughed in response to someone's joke and was quickly informed that a "queen" must never laugh while wearing her crown. With full complement of drums, brass, and dancers we were led to the square from the three-room schoolhouse. There was the usual dancing joy—a little more this time. There were the usual speeches, but now directed to us, and not just welcoming speeches. This is what the Africans had to say to us:

"To speak the truth, the friendly and brotherly attitude you have put up here is of such a nature as not to leave any mark of indifference in the memory of anybody in this town.

"We have often heard people talk of certain racialism in

America, but now without deceit your sojourn among us has clearly proved the great spirit of the American people, and we are sure that racial practices, if they do exist in certain parts of America, have lost ground fast.

"Without flattery we cannot in words express our deep regret at this moment when we are meeting you for the last time. Long live America. Long live Togo. Long live the Afro-American friendship. Good-by."

This tribute to the Crossroaders was written by three Togolese students. One, named Jo, was to leave that month to study at the Patrice Lumumba University in Moscow. Jo would have to sneak across the Ghana border to fly to Russia, because the Russians had refused to offer such scholarships through the Togolese Minister of Education, and the Togolese government was unwilling to give visas to such students contacted directly by the Russians. The fact that the Russians did not require lycée degrees for their university scholarships as the French, Germans, and Americans did was very appealing for a boy who came from a country which had no universities and only one or two lycées. Jo would surely hear the Russians' strongest bid to the Africans against Americans—the case for racial prejudice. The Crossroaders had not gone to Womé to combat communism, but sometimes unconscious accomplishments run deepest. The Russians would not have any easy time convincing Jo that all Americans are a bad lot.

8

Abidjan—
Life in Capital City

A FLUTTER OF FLAGS STRETCHED AS FAR AS YOU COULD SEE—GREEN,
white, and orange stripes—good awning colors. There must have
been eight miles of this material rippling over the avenue from the
airport to Abidjan. It was flying in the smallest alleys and on the
dredges in the harbor. Men wore shirts of it, ladies swung skirts of
it, and children waved their own little flags. Green, white, and
orange. These colors were the only tangible, understandable thing
about independence for most of the people of the Ivory Coast.
The first anniversary of this independence was being celebrated
when I arrived early in August, and the streets were crowded with
dancing groups welcoming visitors for the great event. The presi-
dents from other African countries had come, and Robert Kennedy
and G. Mennen Williams were there from the United States.
Sirens screeched along the highways heralding the approach of
each new very important person.

It was lucky for me that I could stay with the Crossroaders,
because I don't believe there was an extra bed in Abidjan. The

Crossroaders were living in a large, white, airy lycée in Treichville, on the outskirts of Abidjan.

Cathy Cobb greeted me. She had long blond hair pulled back in a bun, light blue eyes, a peaches-and-cream complexion, and delicate features. Botticelli would have looked twice at her. She told me she was attending Pomona College and her home was in South Dakota. She was bubbling with enthusiasm over her summer experiences. She said, "Not many people from South Dakota have been to Africa, and my friends look slightly askance at this venture into the wilds. My family are so eager to hear about Africa that they can't even wait for me to get home and give talks about it. They're already inviting all their friends in to see my slides, and trying to piece them together with my letters."

Since then Cathy has been kind enough to share these letters home with me. I think they deserve circulation beyond the borders of South Dakota as an introduction to the Ivory Coast through the observations of a Crossroader. Even for those familiar with the Ivory Coast, something has been added: it's the Ivory Coast plus Cathy Cobb. Crossroaders have been very generous in sending me their journals and letters home. I only wish it were possible to include more of them in this book. Their reactions and descriptions are all so distinctive that sometimes after reading the letters of three or four in the same group it is hard to realize that they have been exposed to the same experiences. With gratitude to Cathy Cobb, I present excerpts from her very individual journal.

June 29

We are in Africa but we could easily be in a Mediterranean city, or Paris itself. Abidjan is a beautiful, very sophisticated cosmopolitan city. We are fascinated by its complexity but at the same time have been trying to swallow our feelings of disappointment at being on the edge of such a city instead of in the bush. Actually we're situated in Treichville, a transitional section of Abidjan; which is midway between the traditional village society and the sophisticated French city society. We are living in a large

white lycée, and our quarters are quite luxurious compared to some
of our expectations. We were prepared to rough it and we have to
laugh at our sleeping bags all tightly rolled up in a corner. Ann,
Kay, and I have an enormous tile-floored room with three iron cots
and all the little wooden cabinets we can use, since the room was
inhabited by fifty little girls. (The five boys have a similar boudoir
across the hall.) We have 32 sinks, 32 mirrors, 12 showers, and
one john for the three of us. There are no screens to keep out the
wildlife: mosquitoes, lizards, ants, and cockroaches. We keep the
wooden-slatted windows open all the time for the wonderful cool
breeze, and sleep under mosquito nets. All the tight tucking of the
mosquito netting is of no avail if one mosquito gets inside and is
prepared to have his fill on your blood—and how they expand
when they do. The killing of ants isn't so bad; one good lively
dance will finish off almost 10,000 of them.

Our kitchen is a whole building a couple of hundred yards
away. It has an enormous freezer, two sinks, and a tiny gas stove
with an oven. The government has provided us with two wonderful
cooks who bought for a total of 1165f ($3.50) a dinner for ten:
steak, vegetables, potatoes, avocados (beautiful ones), pineapples
(always excellent and very cheap), and bread. The cooks are im-
maculately clean by African standards, but by ours . . . ? We
bought some Ajax and sponges and tried tactfully to tell them that
the table must be wiped off, and cheese put in the refrigerator, and
water boiled twenty minutes, and dishes washed with soap.

The government has also supplied us with a station wagon
and a chauffeur called Michael. Thank heaven for him. He knows
where to take us, what to buy, and he is our lovable link with this
new world.

The first students we've met live nearby the school, attend the
lycée and can discuss Camus, Molière, and classics in beautiful
French. They seem more like black French students than Africans.
About twenty students are eager to work with us—in fact, they
had expected us three days earlier and had been meeting planes

from Monrovia with banners, celebrations, and a planned cocktail party for two days.

July 1

We arose at 5:30 this morning and trudged through mud and rain to the port, where we were to get free shrimp. If you catch the shrimp boats just coming in, they will give each woman, even les étrangers, a basket or bag of fresh shrimp. There were no shrimp, but the fish docks were a new world we wouldn't have missed. Boxes and pans of every size and shape of fish, and crowds of African men and women moving about in the rain, buying and selling the fish, just emptied out of bright blue nets. A fish tied onto the back of a bicycle; a little woman with a baby on her back and a handful of slippery fish for the day's meat; a few all-night dock sleepers yawning and stretching, a giant sea tortoise spouting and flailing on his back; two giant sting rays on the deck, a hammerhead shark pulled in by mistake; and our bedraggled selves in confusion and indecision about which fish are bien à manger . . .

July 2

We just couldn't last out the whole dance last night. It must have gone on until six or seven a.m. This is the last dance because vacations begin now and most of the students will either go back to their villages or stay in Treichville. We're wondering what happens to the student when he goes back into his traditional life and dress for three months; he must feel the contrast very much.

A very "cool" group of students, all especially invited, and beautifully dressed in bright cotton dresses. The girls sit quietly around the rectangular table, while the men seem to circulate. After five hours of dancing we began to recognize the difference between the merengue, the Congolese, the Ivorian dances, and the cha-cha-cha (the Afro-Spanish cha-cha-cha is great). I still feel quite awkward, but one thing we can still dance (unfortunately) is the rock-and-roll, which they demand, not us.

July 4

What a sorry group we are on American Independence Day! Our lack of sufficient sleep, our early-morning marketing on empty stomachs, and too much strange food have caught up with us—four of our group are quite ill. The only reason I'm not is that I went to bed feeling ill and missed supper. I hadn't felt well all day, and, knowing it was just fatigue, I collapsed in bed immediately—only to be awakened a few hours later by three black, very concerned faces, sure that I was really ill, and pressing quinine and Vick's on me. It took a good half hour to persuade them that I didn't have the fever, but it led to a long conversation, a good one, there in our dark dormitory room. One of the students was amazed that American women are so strong when African women are not, and I tried to explain how many years of independence and development had given our women the freedom to work and pursue interests and travel. We talked about the health conditions in Africa. He had had "yellow fever" three times, deplores the filth of the Treichville "hospital," and had never heard of mosquito repellent. I told him that malaria (they just know it as the "fever") had been completely overcome in other parts of the world, but we agreed that it's a most difficult problem in a continent like Africa where malaria will remain as long as there is one mosquito to carry it. We talked about fetishism in the villages—the use of charms instead of physicians to cure diseases—and yet, he said, doctors do visit each village periodically, and the superstition is being overcome.

July 5

We celebrated the 4th (with a few feeble bangs) at the home of the U.S. Ambassador yesterday. What a beautiful home and grounds—recently bush, now cultivated, with a small golf course on the front lawn. Treichville, our world at the moment, is so far removed from an embassy home that we felt a little strange, in spite of the fact that we were with Americans for the first time in two weeks. It was an interesting day, however, and the American

wives were truly interested in Crossroads. One Wellesley graduate was envious of our Treichville life, because it's difficult to see
any Africa from Abidjan. As she said, there is a kind of superficial
veneer over the very integrated African-French city; for the African, generally, is simply not ready to play the twentieth-century
man.

All these people are new to Abidjan. They seem interested in
the real Africa, even though they're not living directly in it.

July 6

Today we visited a little village, Locodjoro, on the edge of
Abidjan, where last year's Crossroaders built a primary school. The
people welcomed us warmly when they found we were also Crossroaders. Locodjoro is a truly tranquil village after noisy Abidjan.
It is right on the edge of a lagoon. The mud-walled, thatch-roofed
houses cluster on the sand, and palm trees grow right up at the
lagoon's edge. Rows and rows of pirogues, the long traditional shell
boats used for fishing and transportation, were lined up between
the palms. Some of us were taken out into the lagoon in pirogues.
There's a real art to paddling these round-bottom, hollowed-out
shells. I tried it alone and found myself paddling in wobbly circles
in the middle of the lagoon.

We've never felt quite so much at home and part of a village
before. There weren't quite the exhausting reception and slightly
superficial festivity, because the village was used to Americans and
knew they would be casual. The children all seemed to be covered
with what looked like white paint—actually it was manioc splashed
all over their bodies. These children proudly showed us inside the
school the Crossroaders had helped them to build last year; and
they showed us letters and photos the group had sent back.

We all loved Locodjoro and kept thinking that if our project
could have been in a village like Locodjoro we could have depth
experience in village life. I'm afraid all American contacts with
villagers are bound to be superficial in some degree—but the degree is smaller if one is living and working there consistently. We

left with the expected hand-shaking, and reluctantly Michael
headed our station wagon back on the forest road.

July 7
Yesterday most of us "buzzed" with the crowd of children
who clustered about us in the school yard, while a few of our men
surveyed. Poor Freddie just can't speak much French, so he's decided to be a clown instead. The children agreed, after gales of
laughter, that all the world—tout le monde comprennent le bouf-
fon! It all became pretty hilarious when Freddie and I decided to
teach them French songs, but all the songs we knew, they had
learned as infants. As we sang "Chevaliers de la Table Ronde,"
they howled and pointed to the primary-school building. The
clowning was really on us!

Our work project is to build a two-room schoolhouse. We have
been delayed for days because of no materials or tools. The Minister of Education, who was to arrange everything for us, has been
in Paris. This morning we finally started to shovel up dirt and grass
for leveling off our site. Two students offered to help us. Otherwise
we don't know where the students are who were to help. We've
heard that they're all in Paris being educated. How great it is to be
working at last if we can just keep from throwing grass in the faces
of our little interested watchers.

July 8
We shopped all morning in the Treichville market. There is
nothing more fun in the world than threading your way through
the melange of color and smells, gingerly stepping over piles of
tomatoes and dried red peppers, trying to avoid putting a foot into
a pan of rice or fresh peanut butter. Each man, woman, and child
seems to have his own pan or basket of something to sell, be it
palm nuts, bread, or husked corn. The manioc dough is spooned
from big pans on the cement into fresh green leaves. Everything
else is somehow wrapped in pieces of discarded brown wrapping

paper. We three American girls were a conspicuous minority among the crowd of brown figures who moved, stooped, and bought in the open market. Children followed us with wide, curious eyes but the women's faces were smoothly impassive. I ventured a smile and a timid "Bonjour, madame," as a woman handed me a bunch of tiny yellow finger bananas. The face that had been cool and impersonal suddenly broke into a grin. She threw her head back and laughed a full delightful laugh as she answered, "Bonjour madame!" to the white face above her. We learned that a bubbling warm humor lies immediately below the surface calm of every African woman.

Freddie, dressed like a traditional African in his pink bedspread, followed us at a safe distance. Freddie's problem was that there's nothing African about him except his color; his robe kept slipping; his step was lively and American; and his mouth kept breaking into a broad grin as he watched us being stared at. It's confusing for many Africans to see either of our Negro boys, because most of them can't conceive of black Americans, yet these boys definitely don't act African. Lennie, our N.Y.U. student and best French speaker because of his year at the University of Lausanne, looks Senegalese (many Senegalese traders on Ivory Coast) so could probably put on a good pose. His French is excellent and we rely on him constantly when we've no idea what's going on.

July 11

Yesterday we really worked—digging the trenches for our building foundations. Ann and I are sitting in the shade near our project surrounded as usual by a crowd of little boys. As we worked yesterday they stood so close to us that we buried their feet in the dirt as we shoveled; they just won't move, even when the shovel handles come close; they are consumed by curiosity over what we are doing. I have about fifteen pairs of black eyes trained on myself and this page right now, and I hear curious murmurs and quiet speculations all about this American girl in pants. It's a little humiliating working out in the blinding sun on a building that the young people know the government could do in nothing flat, on a project that was to have had joint African-American cooperation.

July 12

Mom, this is to you. I had, I think, the happiest experience I've ever had yesterday, not in the organized way we've planned; but we've begun to expect the unexpected. The sun was very hot, and we took turns reading in the shade to a little spontaneous group of African children gathered around us. At first we compared pictures and maps we had of the Ivory Coast and the U.S.A. There must have been over 100 kids, not all of them little. Freddie and I clowned a demonstration of people meeting and saying, "Hello, how are you," etc. There was no need to create gimmicks; they demanded to know words. By the end of the afternoon we would shout or sing up from the trenches we were digging, "Watch your feet," "Watch your nose," as the dirt flew up from our shovels and they all began to shout with us.

Our walk home last night (about two blocks) was a grand procession—each of us surrounded and followed by a group, still demanding to know English words from us. Two small very cute boys had been the quickest of all to learn. They were brothers, Mike and Matu. I said good-by to them with the understanding that I would bring paper and pencil for writing to the work project tomorrow.

After I had been home half an hour, Freddie showed two little visitors into our rooms, Mike and Matu, each with a writing book in hand, asking me to write English words in their notebooks. The three of us sat down on the bed and began to learn the alphabet, their first request. They learned it immediately. Then we wrote the greetings we had been saying that afternoon, and, a little overwhelmed by their brightness and the eagerness that had prompted them to walk all the way home and back to the lycée, I said good-by. You've always said teaching was great, Mom, but you never said it would be like this!

July 13

Again we're waiting for materials. We've dug 4' 15" deep trenches for the foundations of the schoolhouse, but no cement or gravel has come. We went home discouraged about ever finishing the project. And then Mike and Matu walked in the door. They had a list of French phrases for me to translate into English. We had bought three magic slates in Washington. They were an unbelievable invention to these two brothers. They're deceptively small for their eleven and twelve years, but that's because of malnutrition. No one can believe that Freddie and Lennie are twenty-four and twenty-five years; both are large with good-sized muscles.

A really charming young man, whom we had met this morning, came back with six of his friends to find out about the U.S.A. and talk to us. This boy, who is studying to be an artist, just won the prize for the best design for a costume to be worn in one of the Independence Day dances. This is a dance on stilts. Every dance of the Ivory Coast will be performed August 7. Independence came too quickly last year, so there was no chance to plan a celebration. We will be getting in on the first real fête and none of the African students can talk of anything else.

July 14

We still can't work because materials haven't come for cement mixing. We do dig sand out of our six trenches each day. Mike and Matu come regularly for English lessons at 5:30. It's a wonderful experience for me and they're learning a good deal. Learning to speak, read, and write a language all at once is more complicated than I would have thought. It's good there are two of them, because they work on words together at home between lessons. Their parents evidently have sent them to different schools all along. Their home is in a village, and one goes to a primary school there and the other in Abidjan. Modern ideas about independent children! They're fine boys—their family must be a very good one.

July 15

Annette (the sister of our chauffeur, Michael) showed us where to get some African cloth at one of the smaller African markets. Much of it is imported from Holland, and two kinds of durable and less durable from Ghana. Annette knew immediately which cloth was durable and which was not. She handled the whole transaction and we each came away with material for two pagnes, the two pieces of the African women's costume. (Blouse square necked with ruffled waist and skirt a rectangle piece of cloth gathered tightly at the waist like a sarong.) It is incredibly beautiful but we don't have the skin color for this material.

July 16

We had a West African sewing bee today and each of us now has a traditional dress and very lovely ones at that. Annette had promised to help us cut the dresses from the material she helped us pick out. It was our first opportunity to see the inside of a Treichville home. The house seemed to have two rooms plus a little storage room for Michael's motor bike. On the walls were pictures of Mt. Fujiyama and other faraway places, including a photo of American cowboys. The front door opened into a tiled (in bright African colors) front stoop, which faced into an open space. Four or five other tiny houses opened into this space—sharing the kitchen and running water faucet in the center of the courtyard.

We can't communicate with Annette but she loves us and laughs loudly at about everything we do. Without pattern or scissors, just a practiced eye and strong teeth, she ripped and fitted the material. A little lady brought over her Singer machine to help us. In one afternoon we sewed three traditional pagnes—they are very good-looking.

July 23

The project finally has begun to move again! The minister of Education has returned from Paris. At long last we have the supplies we were waiting for—gravel, water for cement, and bricks to begin walls. For two days we've been mixing cement, and it's really backbreaking work.

Ten African students just back from their Paris studies arrived to help us. They aren't exactly typical African students. They are all maturing men of twenty-six or so with pointed leather shoes and dapper suits of the latest Parisian fashion. They don't seem to have much interest in doing construction work and learning about America. But we shall see—they will be an interesting group, and will probably live in our dormitory. It's just that, like much of Abidjan, they are more French than African.

Mike and Matu are wonderful students. I've been wanting to get some African children's drawings, so today I had them draw (with colored chalk I bought) anything that interested them. Mike drew two houses—his family's French house in Treichville and a thatched hut, his home in the village of Gagnoa. Asked which home they preferred, Matu pointed to the more modern edifice, while Mike said that because he was an African he preferred the village home.

July 24

Three of the seemingly mythical twelve African students who arrived from Paris have been working with us. However, their pointed Parisian shoes and good pants just aren't conducive to hard work. One student does work hard though, and asks a good many questions. Lombard is studying engineering in Paris and loves to talk about the night life. Yesterday they asked us about the South and Caryl Chessman. We're amazed at how alive the Chessman case still is—one little boy was reading one of the books Chessman wrote in prison. I've had to find out all about this case long after it happened. There seem to be two questions involved in a Chessman discussion: the justice of capital punishment and the

U.S. legal process that kept Chessman alive so long before he was finally executed. I can't defend the first, but I can point out his appeals as a valuable part of our legal system.

Last night we girls went out to dinner with two Frenchmen. We had a chance to talk about their attitudes toward French Africa and French Africans. There is a marked feeling of superiority over the Africans who go to Paris to adopt French culture and Parisian wives. The Frenchman sees the African as having a super· ficial veneer of sophistication. I think this is true to a small extent, but what we have noticed particularly is that the Africans overdo their Frenchness, so that it is not at all the casual sophistication of the Frenchman. The students we work with seem to deny the existence of a traditional life.

Albert Atcho is a guerisseur, the top spiritual healer of this region. He is not a witch doctor, for his power comes from a Christian God, and not the Devil. The witch doctors dislike him because he takes away their business. He makes a sin of fetishism. He has no medical training and believes that eight out of ten illnesses are psychological and curable. He treats only psychological disorders and does not attempt to cure the really insane. His treatment is based on confession of sins. Each patient writes out a confession and if he isn't cured it is assumed he has not confessed all his sins. We visited his village of Bragbo and had a chance to see some of his patients and see how he heals them. The village started with eighty inhabitants and now the population is three thousand—all patients of the guerisseur. Everyone was dressed in white and the music was loud, nasal calypso chanting. A group of young girls threw leaves and flowers around us, smiling and singing. Albert and a group of elders shook our hands and the women kissed us on both cheeks—a welcome we've never had before. The healer is a huge man treated with the respect and admiration of a king. During our meal with him, the girls who had welcomed us with flowers hovered over him to wipe the sweat from his brow and to pour him fresh water. After an excellent dinner we were taken on a tour of the village. There was no hospital as such; the whole village was his place of treatment. One area had several men and women chained to trees. They were guilty of fetishism and had not been able to confess their sins. This chaining was standard treatment. When they finally confessed, they would be released and, amazingly enough, they would get well. We saw a pile of the fetishes (bottles, padlocks, sticks, etc.) which had been confiscated from the guilty ones and would be burned at the end of the year. Besides these fetish crimes, Albert's other specialty is curing women who believe themselves barren. Apparently he is very successful, but of course he always has the loophole of saying that the ones who are not cured have not confessed their sins. You're the psychologist, Dad, so you know more about curing people by giving them a sense of security and freedom from guilt.

July 25

Houphouet-Boigny returned from Paris yesterday morning. His arrival is well timed just before Independence Day. We all left work (as did the rest of Treichville and Abidjan) to see his grand reception at the port. His boat, decked with flags, was pulled alongside the dock, and crowds of thousands lined the way. A band, the first organized musical group I've seen here, was ready to play, and all the important chiefs in the area, dressed in beautiful robes, were lined up to receive him. There are times that it's great to be an American! We told the official guards that we were the American delegation and should be allowed to enter. They looked a little skeptical, but what could they say! So we stood right behind the Ministers of State and the Big Chiefs. Houphouet-Boigny is a short, very dignified middle-aged man with an attractive twenty-year-old wife. While groups of African women danced and beat rhythm sticks, Houphouet-Boigny got into a large limousine and was driven off to his fantastic new marble palace.

August 1

It has become impossible to do any work on our seven-foot-high walls, because Independence Day is taking over our school yard! Yesterday afternoon, mammy wagons started rolling into the yard, bringing loads of people from interior villages, who are going to stay in the school rooms during these exciting days of the celebration. The wagons are packed full. Evidently, a pretty select group is sent from each village; each sends its best dance group and a number of other villagers. The most exciting part of this whole thing is that the dancers come dressed, and the minute they pile off the truck the musicians get situated, a large circle of village people, curious children, and more curious Crossroaders forms, and they practice their dance right there. The first group that arrived was dressed in short, full straw skirts, with jangling pieces of metal tied around their ankles, and elaborate straw headdresses. Another group had short pieces of a lovely blue cotton material wrapped around their muscular legs. And how they dance . . . the acrobatics, and the skilled muscular control that goes into these movements are unlike anything we've ever seen.

It reminds me that we teach our children syncopation so carefully in grade school, so that they'll understand the somewhat difficult process of singing a rhythm which is not exactly "on the beat." Syncopation would be a meaningless word in these people's vocabulary, because all their rhythm is so complex; simultaneously, four, five, and six beat patterns may form the background for a dance. You can imagine the type of body movement necessary to match this intricate, intense rhythm.

The first group who drove in, piling out their women with their sleeping mats and small cook stoves, their bright-colored dancers, and drummers, were all elderly people, and we wondered if all the people who came from the villages would be old. Perhaps only the old could have the privilege of responding to the invitation of the President of Ivory Coast to come from all over the country to the I-D celebration. Or perhaps it is only the older people who maintain the traditional dances any more, as more and more young people are receiving a western-oriented education. Our questions were answered by the arrival of the second group, a dance group of very young, attractive men, with acrobatic ability that amazed us.

We left our trowels, and our wheelbarrows full of mortar, and watched each group practicing. There was such variety in the individual dances. We watched a dance of sorcery from up in a tree. Everette nearly fell out into the dance circle, trying to lean out far enough for a good picture of these women, dressed all in white, carrying fetishes, and dancing a mournful, slow dance. There was slight dissension among our ranks, because a couple of the group thought we should continue building in spite of the dancers. I was not among the group that thought we should put away our cameras and curiosity and get back to work. Only once in our life probably will we be able to watch Ivory Coast traditional dances from a distance of 8 feet. Dances we couldn't have seen by traveling in the interior for five years, because they are special, and not shown to passers-by. So Everette and I stayed up in the tree, rebellious, to watch!

August 2

When we arrived on the project early this morning, there on the cement place where we usually stand to get water for mixing mortar were several elderly women, doing their morning laundry. They were using a great deal of soap, so that suds covered everything, and most of them used their feet for scrubbing, and sudsing the clothing; more than their hands. It was truly wash day, for several were washing themselves as well as the family clothing.

Our university students are not working very much this last week, because, we're told, they're practicing for the parade. Only François works steadily, singing French songs all the time, and we enjoy him and the fact that he is the steadiest worker of the African group. We were prepared for the fact that the university student in Africa is a very important person. He belongs to a small select group of the young people who have been able to graduate from the lycée, and whose education in France is wholly financed by the Ivory Coast government. These ten students who were flown back to work with us are the doctors, lawyers, architects, engineers, and statesmen of about two years from now, and physical labor is about the farthest possible thing from their interest. Thus, the fact that a number of them did work fairly hard on the project is gratifying. Felix, the medical student, who loves Spanish poetry and Russian dancing, and wears a black Cossack hat with his traditional robe, was really my favorite, not because he worked hard (because he usually lay on the sand pile, gazing at the clouds, smoking his pipe) but because we had good conversations about the health problems of the Ivory Coast, about fetishism, and politics. He has less of the "French veneer" which seems so artificial to us, and which seems so much a part of some of the other students. Felix, in spite of his goatee and pipe, is genuinely concerned about making a medical contribution to Ivory Coast. He became engaged to an African girl soon after he arrived in Abidjan—an important thing, because many of the students feel African women aren't educated and sophisticated enough for them, after their French schooling, and often marry French girls, who have no interest in living in Africa.

I have no idea what sort of impression we have made on these students. I think they like us personally fairly well, but continue to feel vastly superior because of the French culture and sophistication which is such a part of them. They were surprised at our being there, and our willingness to do this kind of labor in spite of the fact that we are students; and they are particularly doubtful about why we girls are here. One morning I was called over to explain why we girls came on such a project. I think the fact that we mixed cement, laid bricks, and shoveled quantities of dirt persuaded them that we were there to work and understand, rather than just to keep up the spirits of the group. There was no great feeling of sadness when we finished our last day of work with the university students, though I was sorry to say good-by to Felix and to François's songs. We were, however, glad that three weeks of our summer were spent in trying to become acquainted with these students, because they are our peers, and will be in the same relative positions as the fellows in our group will be in a few years. One would think that the educated of two very different countries would find the most in common, and in some sense we did, because we were able to discuss intelligently the Berlin and Cuban situation, U.S. integration, and Ivory Coast problems in a way that we couldn't do with secondary school students who were around us all the time. It's with the educated groups, however, that national pride interferes. We're part of a country whose strength and whose culture are established and accepted, but these students have a double dose of national pride because their country is so new, and they have to believe in its potential for recognition by the rest of the world very strongly. Thus, they were not as anxious as we to act as peers. This part of the project, gaining some kind of rapport with the university students, was not at all easy, but if we had never come in contact with this segment of the Ivory Coast population we would have avoided one of the most important, influential parts of the country's future.

August 8

These past two days of Independence Day celebration have been exhausting, and not quite as exciting as all the preparation that led up to them. We have been watching dances in our school yard, watching the primary school students (including Matu and Mike) practicing gymnastics for the big day, and each night after dinner we walk out into the Treichville streets, following the sounds of singing and drums to their source. There are so few electric lights that it's like feeling our way through a dark cave to get through the back streets to a place where a dance is going on. Everette and I followed an intriguing drum rhythm through the streets for a long time before we found it last night. Finally we ended up in the school yard where our project is, and there a Bete group was practicing a family sort of dance. That is, young and old, mother and children, and mothers with children-on-the-way were doing a circle dance, and somehow I got drawn into it and enjoyed myself thoroughly.

The next day the celebration began, and the city of Abidjan was wholly alive with the excitement. Annette, who is the sister of our government-supplied chauffeur Michael (who is definitely "one of the family" now) and who helped us to sew African dresses last week, persuaded us that we should wear them on Independence Day—so we did! And what an experience. No Europeans care about imitating African traditional dress, so with our very white skins, blond hair, and bright cotton garb we were an unusual sight. We wondered if our costuming would be interpreted negatively, because we love the dress, and wanted to show our African friends that we enjoy identifying with them even though the absurdity of the identification is obvious. To our relief, everyone we met was delighted (that is putting it mildly) with the dress—especially the women, for which we were especially glad. Choruses of "C'est joli!" and "C'est bon, ca!" followed us, and we got our pictures taken several times—which was a turnabout. We walked into the stadium to watch our primary school friends' gymnastics program, the children, who had been practicing for two months in our school yard and knew us, were lined up ready to march out onto the field. When they saw us in African dress they gave a roaring unison shout—a little embarrassing! We didn't intend to cause a sensation, but couldn't seem to avoid it! The climax of this whole thing occurred when Everette and I walked home from the big parade on the bridge, which had consisted of marching groups of school children dressed in bright uniforms and new shoes (government-bought) and veterans of the two world wars. A tall, extremely stately African man in a gold traditional robe stopped and greeted us in a very friendly way. He shook Everette's hand, then turned to me, indicated the dress, said, "C'est bonne, madame," and "Excusez-moi, monsieur" to Everette (thinking he was my husband), then turned back to me and gave me a big kiss on the cheek. All three of us were pleasantly astonished. . . .

The following afternoon we watched the village dances in the stadium, or rather, they were performed in the stadium, but the field was a mass of black faces and a cloud of dust hovered over everything, and though we knew that somewhere out there the dances we had watched for a week in our school yard were being danced, it was impossible to see them. The President's (of the U.S.) brother, Robert Kennedy, and his wife were the official delegation from the U.S. at the celebration—they too strained to see into the dust and mass of people, but must have failed.

August 12

Today we leave Treichville, and I wonder how at home we have become here in our six-week stay. The main thought on our minds is relief that we will be leaving our quarters, mainly because privacy is a nonexistent thing—each morning our little friends come into see us, usually peering right into our mosquito-net tents to say "Bonjour!" in spite of the fact that we are obviously sound asleep. We are always willing to spend this time with children, because it's our one opportunity to give some information back to these people who have given so much to us this summer; nevertheless, we're very tired, and will be glad to have a change by beginning our three-week travel period.

It hasn't been easy to make real friends during this period; it's been a breadth rather than a depth of acquaintances, because so many students come sporadically to visit us, not regularly, and most of them are quite a bit younger than we. Matu and Mike are an exception to all this—I feel that of all the African young people we've known during this period, they are the two that I feel close to, and am going to miss genuinely. They aren't "two little African boys" . . . they are just two real people who've spent a great deal of time with us, not only in the English lessons I've helped them with, but at meal times, or evening visits, when they just come to be around the group. If they are examples of the kind of young people who are growing up in this different time in Africa's history, one can be somewhat encouraged about the quality of leadership which might be a part of the country's development.

Our seven feet of cinder block wall isn't as impressive as the nearly-finished projects of many of the groups, but for the type of situation we have been in, I don't think it matters at all. Unlike the Ghana group working at Nkwatia, we are not building a school in a community that couldn't, probably, build its own building. The government of Ivory Coast could have raised a primary building in a week, while it took us six to do these bare walls. Part of the adjustment to our project experience was (had to be) our eventual acceptance of the fact that we were not particularly indispensable to Treichville—on the contrary, we looked ridiculous mixing cement by hand, digging trenches for the foundation, when machines of this modern city could have done it. We were sincerely humiliated our first day—but our state of mind changed when we realized that, by being in a city, we were in the center of the Africa that is growing and changing, and slowly developing into a modern society. We couldn't have gotten the wide variety of points-of-view we've gotten: of educated Africans, government officials, writers of the country, uneducated men and women, university and college students, French residents of Abidjan, African women and young girls, if we had been in a remote village. Realizing this, we eventually decided to forget that we weren't really needed in Treichville, and set about to know as many of the elements of this French-built city as possible.

As a result of all this, our barely-begun building is the least important part of the summer—it just represents a fairly effective means for us to be right in the center of a transitional African community. Thank goodness the "success" of our summer didn't depend on the size of the actual building we put up with such inexperienced hands, but on the kind of contacts we were slowly able to make with the people of Treichville.

Pomona College
Claremont, California
February 5, 1962

Dear Mrs. Plimpton:

In answer to your question "How has Crossroads changed my life?"

Well, I'm Africa-conscious, which I certainly was not a year ago. I notice everything that is said and written about the continent, search for African music, have made the effort to become well acquainted with the two African students at Pomona (our first), when I might have found myself "too busy" two years ago. I have a new "group" of friends, which is scattered all over the country, all very different people, but all with this same experience in common—we are all, also, a part of a much larger group which consists of anyone who feels a great interest in Africa. Personally, a great many things about the summer, mostly relationships with the African people we knew, and especially with members of the Ivory Coast group have taught me a great deal about my own abilities and reactions. I've become sensitive to the Southern integration problem (something for which a Midwesterner usually has little real feeling), as a result of having two Negro friends (the first I have had) in my own group, and also as a result of knowing the feelings of the white Southerner in our group. I watch and listen for news of the Southern problem in a way which is quite different from what I did before.

I find myself doing a great deal of public speaking again, something I enjoyed immensely in high school, but had done little of since—and I love it, because it's revived an ability I didn't think I had any more. Something else which is important, I think, is that at the same time that I feel as though I have a considerable amount of knowledge about something which few people have been able to experience in the way we were able to be part of an African community, I also came away with the feeling one usually gets in "digging" into a new field—that your experience, more than giving you "knowledge," really just reveals your own ignorance to yourself, and makes you wary of answering questions with any sort of absolute answers. We found out that Africa, or Ivory Coast, or Treichville, or whatever, is complex above all.

I want to go back to Africa very much in order to carry through the introduction to the continent (which is all a summer can be) into something more. I've applied for the Peace Corps, which would be the most valid way to (for me) get back to Africa as something more than a tourist; but I want some teacher training before I go back—because at this point, I would be going back to give myself experience, or maybe an experience, rather than as a trained person who can contribute something. All I can do is plan my life one year at a time right now—and I'll probably be in the Yale or Radcliffe Master of Art in Teaching program next year, which would lead to Peace Corps or something similar the following year. In this state of "senior uncertainty" I would be dishonest if I said "I am going to . . ." do anything.

Yours truly,
Cathy Cobb

9

Liberia—
Teaching Project

How would you go about teaching children geography without a map? History without books? Arithmetic without a blackboard? Biology without a lab? How would you make things stick without glue? How would you make things bright without paint? These were a few of the many questions that confronted the eight trained Crossroads teachers who went to Liberia last summer to teach school. It was quite different from the work-project experience of all the other Crossroaders. This was an older group of graduate trained teachers. It was a novel experience for them, coming as they did from schools that enjoy the most up-to-date equipment and latest teaching techniques. They had a good chance to test out their ingenuity in this new setting. Instead of receiving a salary for their professional performance in a strange country, devoid of equipment and lacking in program, they were paying for the privilege of an adventure in teaching unlike anything they could find at home. They were in the strange predicament of being Americans teaching Africans to teach Africans. Quite unconsciously the African teachers were also teaching American teachers many things they would bring home to American children.

The very name Liberia and the motto of the country, "The love of liberty brought us here," led me to anticipate a country that showed the advantages of its long-standing freedom and association with the United States. Monrovia was founded as a settlement for the repatriation of freed American slaves in 1822, and in 1847 Liberia became the first independent African country. The Americo-Liberians who founded the Republic and formed the ruling class had never experienced freedom themselves. They ruled the indigenous people of Liberia much the same way they had been treated as cotton pickers in southern United States. The country had missed the spirit and inspiration which we like to think of as American.

Coming to Monrovia was a distinct letdown after the more glamorous capitals of Nairobi, Salisbury, Brazzaville, Lagos, Accra, and Abidjan. It gave me a much greater appreciation of the constructive parenthood of the colonial powers. Not only had they left beautiful buildings in many of the capital cities, but they had left a very good educational structure to build on.

In the British colonies the London system was used as a standard for all the colleges. In many cases, such as the University of Rhodesia and Nyasaland in Salisbury, the standards seemed a little high, for the college was only half full. However, independent countries such as Ghana and Nigeria were adjusting the British system of education to fit the African needs. No matter what the adjustments, there was a distinct advantage to having a good backbone as a starter. This was what Liberia lacked. The United States missed one of the greatest opportunities it ever had in failing to spend money to build a topnotch educational system there.

Until fairly recently, a good part of Liberia's educational funds, instead of being invested on the home front for one and all, were used to send the children of the ruling class abroad for their education—even at the primary level. Tubman is the first

president to recognize the educational needs of the indigenous people of the interior and express the desire to do something about
them. There are 30,000 Liberian children who have never been to
school. Although a law has been passed making education compulsory for all children, it is impossible to enforce because of lack
of teachers. This is not unique in Liberia. One of the greatest vacu-
ums throughout Africa is the scarcity of teachers, particularly on
the secondary-school level. Many of the existent Liberian teachers
are also sadly lacking in training.

The Liberian Department of Public Instruction has created
Extension Schools and Vacation Schools to help further the education of these teachers. Each teacher is compelled to attend one
or the other. The Extension Schools meet in the evenings during
the school year and the Vacation Schools during the holidays.
Last year the Department of Public Instruction, realizing the need
for more modern methodology, tried a new experiment. They invited Operation Crossroads Africa to send trained teachers to in-
struct the Liberian teachers in their Vacation Summer School.
Although foreign missionaries had held schools for Liberian children, this was the first time that any volunteer teachers had come
from abroad for the express purpose of helping the Liberian teachers. The Crossroad teachers had no idea how they would be received by the government or by the local teachers. It was an
experiment for Crossroads as well as the Liberian Department of
Public Instruction.

The first sign of approval was President Tubman's complete
backing of the program. He budgeted enough money to pay for the
living and traveling expenses of these eight Crossroads teachers
and their leader, Dr. Clarence Jayne.

The eight Crossroads teachers arrived in Monrovia for a short
briefing. Then they split up in teams of two to go in relays to eight
centers (at Harper, Greenville, Buchanan, Monrovia, Robertsport,
Bomi Hills, Gbaranga, and Zorzor) to conduct teaching workshops
for one week in each place. Those Liberian teachers living within
commuting distance of one of these areas were asked to attend. It

was anticipated that about 600 of the 2000 eligible teachers would be able to get to the seminars. Men left their farms and women their families to come. Many had to walk for two, three, or even four days (at a rate of about twenty-five miles a day) to get to these conferences. The government allocated fifty cents a day to each of the teachers for food, but they had no idea where they were going to eat or sleep when they left home. To the amazement of everyone, 1551 teachers (out of the possible 2000) attended the Crossroads seminars.

The Crossroads teacher team was really challenged to know how to use each allotted week in the best possible way. The Liberian teachers were not familiar with the art of discussion as a means of teaching, since their experience had been limited to the field of questions to which there was only one acceptable *right* answer. Through the workshop approach the Crossroads teachers steered the Liberian ones away from the rote method of teaching and introduced the unit method of developing a lesson. Each Crossroader had her own way of working out her subject matter in conjunction with the Liberian teachers.

Hazel Cox describes one of her projects:

A unit on the first Liberian flag was developed. The teachers did research for background emphasis. They were then introduced to motivation through storytelling. Following this means of motivation they engaged, to their delight, in dramatizing the story of the making of the first Liberian flag. The idea was so new and the simple dramatization so appealing that from that day on Student T. was addressed as "President Roberts" and Student D. as "Susannah Lewis," both comparable in Liberian history to the Father of our Country and Betsy Ross. It was here and in their singing that I first realized the great talents hidden within the people of Liberia. Then followed a letter-writing activity, for July 26 would be Liberia's Independence Day. This activity emphasized new vocabulary learnings. It integrated reading, spelling, the mechanics of handwriting, and sentence structure. For appropriate music they taught me their glorious Liberian Anthem and a little song about their flag. Crafts integrated counting and measurement in making individual Liberian flags. The culmination of the unit was a parade on the campus grounds and picture taking.

Other teachers used the unit system for making studies of nature, literature, music, and tribal customs. They were particularly interested in exploring Liberian heritage. In one lesson the Liberian teachers brought in leaves and herbs from the area and explained how they were used in medicine and ointments. They had charming legends and stories to tell, and the Crossroads teachers learned many of their folk songs and dances. Several of the Crossroads teachers used poems from the *African Treasury*, edited by Langston Hughes, as a springboard for lessons in creative writing or drawing.

The great outdoors was the main supply room for these teaching projects. One could make wonderful maps in mud. Bulletin boards were put together with bamboo strips. Paste was concocted of latex from the nearby rubber trees mixed with a little gasoline. The juice from certain trees made good paint. So did the red clay. Hard seeds were handy for counting games. Sand was available for clay modeling, and wood for carving. Bottle tops plus cardboard circles made good tambourines, and bottle tops plus match boxes made nice little cars. Jump ropes could be made by stripping leaves off the beach rope. There were endless things to be done with the material on hand. Most of the schoolhouses had been built with twigs, vines, and mud.

The Liberian teachers had to work under crowded conditions. In some schools the children had to wait out in the hall, taking their turns in the classrooms. In some classes there was an age range from five to fifteen years. Chairs were scanty and desks a luxury. Despite all these handicaps, the Liberian teachers seemed remarkably able to hold the attention of their children.

There was a good deal of talk about discipline. Being late for school was one of the punishable crimes. The Liberians became interested in discussing the alternatives to corporal punishment, and "Firm but fair" became the byword. The idea of a PTA was introduced as a method to get parents to cooperate in helping their children get off to school on time.

As Liberian children often came to school hungry, one of the Liberian teachers' problems was to devise ways of supplementing inadequate home diets. Some of them grew vegetable gardens. This didn't answer everything, though. In one instance the all-powerful village chief sold the school vegetable garden for a case of whisky.

The Crossroaders were able to present the Meals for Millions program in many places where it might be adopted. This is a non-profit program developed by General Mills. Its purpose is to supplement the local diets in areas where food is deficient in protein as well as certain vitamins and minerals. A specially developed meal made from concentrated soybeans costs three cents for two ounces and contains adequate nutrients for one person for one day. This can be added to any native food without violating religious or dietary habits. Meals for Millions volunteers to send an experimental ton of this concentrate to aid any country with responsible leadership desiring to accept the program.

The secondary schools had more problems. Some of the pupils were self-supporting adults who were as old as their teachers and often earned more money. Some of the younger pupils were boarding in the towns without any adult supervision. They came from very different educational backgrounds. Those who had been to missionary schools knew Latin, while others scarcely knew English. Everywhere there was the problem of finding the appropriate space, light, and privacy to study. Books and magazines were practically nonexistent in bushtowns. The Crossroads teachers discussed the possibilities of using the USIS National Library, the Airline Offices, the Embassies, and ICA for information.

Outside speakers could also help keep them informed. Jane Martin invited the director of the audio-visual department in Monrovia to come and talk to one of her classes. His hobby was exploring historical sites. The Liberian teachers became so interested that they invited him back to talk to their classes, and several of them took up exploring on their own.

One of the Liberian teachers remarked to a Crossroads teacher at the end of their teaching session, "The most important thing I have gained from this week was the feeling that other people like yourself have a respect for things that are African." Africans have been haunted by the feeling that their local traditions were considered "uncivilized" in a very "civilized" world. Many of the young, on receiving an education, flee from what they consider to be their uncivilized communities to the supposedly civilized center of Monrovia. The Crossroaders tried to impart the thought that "the culture of a people is the sum total of the way people have learned to get along in their environment."

One of the great challenges in Liberia today is how to inspire the educated youth so that they will not separate from their homes, but realize the value of applying what they have learned in their own communities.

The Crossroaders were not at all sure that anything could be accomplished by them in such a short time. They knew that more "teachers of teachers" and more time were badly needed. The response to their efforts was most heart-warming.

A typical response to the Crossroads teaching project was expressed by the Superintendent of Schools in Harper City when he wrote his report to the Secretary of Education in Monrovia. He said:

Never have we experienced so lively a five days of living together and learning together as these. Our attendance was record-breaking. The sessions were never too long and the hours went by with great velocity, usually the case with teachers, and the parting pathetic and filled with emotions. . . .

We feel confident that the impression made on this group will remain ever green in their minds and serve as a sufficient encouragement for a continuous program of the Operation Crossroads Africa, and an understanding of our ambitions and aspirations of the teachers and the hope engendered for the future of children and Liberia. . . .

One of the principles of the Crossroads teacher which we very highly appreciated was that she did not put on any air of superiority with us. She gave us to understand that she came out to share with our experience—to learn from us as we learned from her. It is our prayer that our paths would cross again and that their stay might be longer.

The Liberian government was so delighted with the success of this project that they requested that thirty-six teachers (one music teacher, seven junior and senior high-school teachers, twenty-six elementary-school teachers and two kindergarten teachers) be sent to teach at next year's Vacation Schools. In order to meet the Crossroads schedule, the entire school calendar for Liberia will have to be shifted around. It is indeed a tribute to Crossroads that the Liberian government feels strongly enough to make this adjustment.

When I joined this group of Crossroaders they had finished their teaching projects and were planning to spend the remaining few weeks traveling. I accompanied them on a trip into the interior of Liberia. We left Monrovia in two cars on a paved road which continued inland as far as President Tubman's estate. After the "Coo Coo Nest," the name given to President Tubman's guest house, the road was unpaved. From there on it was like a steady trot, but too unpredictable to do any posting. I was riding with Joe Morris, the Director of Teacher Education, who was responsible for all the planning for the Crossroaders in Liberia. He suggested that we stop in the next village, Gbandilla, which was like many others we had passed, with a predominance of mud huts. We drew up alongside a whitewashed house called "Stuarts." We were ahead of the other busload of Crossroaders. When Joe suggested that we order hamburgers for everyone to save time, I thought to myself that a summer with Americans was really starting to tell on him, if he could make this Howard Johnson kind of joke in a remote African village. Not at all; we were served hamburgers which competed favorably with any of Mr. Johnson's. You never could tell when or where a taste of America would turn up in this country.

Next to the restaurant was another whitewashed building, beside which the Liberian flag was flying merrily. This was the local school, and it was in session. Charline Charot thought she'd take a look at the classroom after lunch, and I followed her. The minute she stepped inside the little white schoolhouse, there was an explosion of greetings. The teacher dropped everything to greet her friend from the Vacation School. This was a one-room schoolhouse, rather dark inside, since there were windows on only one side and blackboards on the other three walls. Several rows of benches faced each of the blackboards. These were three classes, each facing its respective blackboard and backing the center of the room. The two teachers were giving lessons to two of the groups, while the third group waited patiently for its turn. The children looked shiny clean in their faded khaki school uniforms. The first teacher clasped Charline's hand and pointed above the rows of wide-eyed children to something dangling from the ceiling. "Look, look," she said. "We've done it already!" The object suspended by a piece of raffia from the rafters was obviously an automobile, made of bamboo cut into small parts and intricately pieced together; even its headlights and wheels were made of bamboo. The proud creator of this object was asked to stand to receive our compliments on his workmanship. The real cause for the teacher's rejoicing was her pride in showing that she had already put to practice some of the things she had learned in Charline's class at the Vacation School. She had stimulated her pupils to create their own toys with the imaginative use of the indigenous materials around them.

This was not the only warm reception I witnessed while traveling with these eight teachers. Everywhere we went, at every school we neared, a broadly grinning African teacher would come running out to hail her former Crossroads teacher and then proudly show off her rows of small beaming pupils. It was hard to believe that this group of Crossroaders could have become so well-known and well-loved throughout the country in one short summer.

We visited the Zorzor Training Center, where two of the Crossroaders had held one of their seminars. This was a beautiful school, just opened, with all the latest equipment; it had been built by AID for $30,000 where there used to be nothing but bush. The purpose of the school was to train African students to teach elementary school. One hundred such students came from all parts of Liberia and boarded at the school for two years while they pursued their studies. Tuskegee College had sent six teachers on a professional contract. A demonstration school for teachers was being built nearby, which would be attended by the children of the neighboring village. Mr. William Pollard, the headmaster, showed us his farm, which was being used as an educational project for the whole village. They were cultivating rice fields and planning a fish pond. Another project was crossing African pigs with New Hampshire pigs. We were served a delicious home-grown supper that night.

AID is planning to build several similar teacher training centers in other parts of Liberia. Crossroads had the satisfaction of dovetailing nicely with the ICA program.

On the way to visit the newly discovered Nimba ore mines, we stopped at the neighboring town of Sanniquellie, where I saw one of the nicest sights of all. Opposite the church and next to the school was a three-room library, built by the 1960 Crossroaders and recently painted pink and blue with yellow trim. The whole town, in fact, had a fresh bright look, as it was considered compulsory for everyone to give his home a new coat of paint in honor of President Tubman's anticipated visit in a few weeks to dedicate the Crossroads Library and a new marketplace. The library was still empty, but this would not be for long. The 1960 Crossroaders had collected 100,000 books, which they had sent to Liberia. A vague count of the number of books in the major libraries would suggest that this gift more than doubled the number of books already in the whole country. These books were not all to be used at the Sanniquellie Library, but were to be shared by others.

An excerpt from a Monrovia daily paper, *The Listener,* Friday, February 16, 1962, describes the Liberian reaction to the arrival of 150,000 more books the following year:

The Liberian people, particularly school children, teachers, and administrators, have expressed gratitude for a shipment of book gifts from America which have arrived in Monrovia.

The books, numbering over 150,000 volumes of all sorts (approximately 25 tons) arrived by the African Patriot, sailing from New York.

They were carefully selected from donors in the United States and Canada, and will be distributed in libraries throughout Liberia.

This collection of books is a continuation of the work of the Liberia group of Operation Crossroads Africa of 1960, which built a library on the grounds of the Central School at Sanniquellie.

At first the effort was centered around filling this library building for the use of the students, faculty, and townspeople of Sanniquellie, but the project gained such momentum because of the speeches made by Dr. James Robinson, director of Crossroads, and by other members of the Liberia group of 1960 that the number and variety of books collected make it possible to give books to other libraries, such as the University of Liberia and the High School at Cape Palmas.

The various groups of people who have worked on the project cannot express their immense satisfaction which the success of the project has afforded them.

By every group the books have been collected, packed, and delivered, with loving zeal, to the pier of the Farrell Lines, which is generously transporting the books free of charge to Monrovia. The project is an outgrowth of the person-to-person relationship

which was started in the summer of 1960, but which is not termi-
nated in a brief summer. It represents rather a life-long interest
in a sister country whose interests are now our own.

The 1961 Crossroaders also had plans for continuing their project in Liberia after they returned to the United States. These teachers were returning to various schools that were eager to learn about Africa. Having made personal contacts and compiled lists of very definite needs, they were in a position to supervise communication between Liberian and American school children.

They knew just which school supplies would be most appropriate and useful to send where. They knew how much it would mean to those isolated centers of learning like Zorzor to receive any kind of magazine subscription which would help keep them in contact with the world at large. The brand-new library at Zorzor was still barren of books. The library at the University of Liberia in Monrovia was quite inadequate (about 10,000 books). The Booker T. Washington Institute for technical training under the dynamic leadership of Moses K. Weefur also needed books. Cuttington College had the best library. The Crossroaders knew the names and addresses of the schools which needed globes, blackboards, books, and visual aids so desperately. They could return to the United States with information for those at home who would like to participate in some small constructive way in the exciting development of education in Liberia.

Crossroaders are two-way operators of communications between people on the African and American sides of the Atlantic: people who seek communication so that they may learn something; and people who, because they have learned something, seek further communication.

10

Mr. Quaidoo and Ghana

THE HONORABLE P. K. K. QUAIDOO'S HOUSE WAS IN COMPLETE CON-
trast to its surroundings. It was an impressive villa glowing in the
moonlight like a beacon commanding the surrounding country-
side. As I climbed the hill leading up to it, I asked the Crossroaders if the villagers didn't resent this show of wealth, and was
quickly told that Mr. Quaidoo was revered and esteemed by the
entire community. They were very proud of his political and financial success, which exceeded anything they had ever known or
dreamed of. They were grateful that, although Mr. Quaidoo had
gone to England for his education and had lived in Accra, the
capital of Ghana, as an active member of Parliament and of
Nkrumah's Convention Peoples' Party, he had not forgotten the
people of his own home town, Gyaamen. As Minister of Social Welfare and Community Development, Mr. Quaidoo had
used his influence to interest the government in supporting the
model village on which the Crossroaders were working. Papayebre
Village, as it was called, was the inspiration of Mr. Quaidoo, and
quite the most exciting project that had ever taken place in this
district.

As we approached the courtyard of the villa, I asked Tony Blackburn, the Crossroads leader, how this man had accumulated so much wealth. Tony explained that Quaidoo's father had been the village chief, and with vast amounts of land at his disposal had been able to cultivate Ghana's main crop, cocoa.

We walked through the courtyard, fragrant with flowers, and through a stylish, comfortable living room onto a balcony. Mr. Quaidoo was waiting for us, a tall, well-built man, about forty-five years old, in Western dress. After a warm greeting he offered me a seat.

As he poured out a gin and tonic, he said, "I am working on a new law that I want to get passed in Ghana."

"Really?" I said, hoping to learn something.

"Yes." He twinkled. "I want to pass a law forbidding all Crossroaders ever to leave Ghana."

Although I had every intention of taking an objective look at the Crossroads program, I couldn't ignore the trickles of happiness I felt every time something was added to my collection of Crossroads compliments.

Egging him on, I asked, "Have the Crossroaders fitted into your community plan?"

"Perfectly," he said. "I can't imagine anything that could have given more of a boost to our project than the participation of the Crossroaders. Such genuine interest from the outside couldn't help but encourage the spirit of community self-help which we are trying to stimulate in these small villages. The fact that the Africans are not working *for* the Crossroaders but *with* them gives them added incentive. The fact that the Crossroaders have paid, instead of being paid, to come and work with the Africans is a proof of their sincerity and true interest in African problems."

I noticed a chart lying on the table, marked "Papayebre Village," and asked if I could look at the plans. Mr. Quaidoo pointed out the locations for a community center, a church, a library, a clinic, a post office, stores, and a section for homes. Rising to his feet, he said, "Come and look out over the layout for the village."

I followed my host to the edge of the circular balcony, which was attractively illuminated by indirect lighting. We were up just high enough to get a lovely, hazy view of the surrounding country-side, just visible in the pale moonlight. An area of about forty acres had been cleared away for the proposed village, and beyond was the deep, dark bush.

Mr. Quaidoo looked over the landscape dreamily. "It will take several years before we can complete the village," he said, "but we're off to a good start with three buildings already finished. When the Crossroaders arrived we started on a fourth."

"Which are the three?" I asked rather stupidly, not having quite grasped the general layout of the village.

Mr. Quaidoo laughed. "You are visiting one right now—the home of the local M.P." I knew "military police" wasn't relevant here and had to think a minute before I realized that he meant Member of Parliament.

"You're living in another of the buildings," he added, gesturing toward the quadrangle of four school buildings below. Although school was in session, Mr. Quaidoo had arranged to have the Crossroaders take over one of the four. "I built this primary school for the community. There has been a great need for such schools in our country. There has been much improvement in the four and a half years since we have had independence. Almost one hundred per cent of the children attend primary school (first four grades) now, while formerly only about twenty per cent went to school at all. Our bottleneck is with the secondary school. We don't have the trained teachers, but that is where the Peace Corps will be helping us out."

I remarked that I had admired many new school buildings, driving from Accra to Gyaamen.

"The third building I was going to tell you about," he said, "is another one of my pet projects. See that long, narrow building over to the right. That is my shirt factory. I want to introduce light industry into the community. As soon as we can build enough roads, I intend to add other light industries of a similar nature, starting first of all with the making of articles of clothing, and, after a few years, adding to this the manufacture of light machinery parts, when enough schooled technicians are turned out of the University College of Science and Technology in Kumasi to make this feasible. I hope that this basic light industry, together with the cocoa farms in the surrounding area, will give the village a reasonable standard of living and enable it to be self-supporting."

I asked Mr. Quaidoo whether he got much profit from his shirt factory.

He chuckled. "You'd be amazed to see how much the output has increased since I divided the workers into two competitive teams. I am saving all my gains from the shirt factory to be left to the town of Papayebre, and when I die the factory will also belong to the town."

I was still puzzled as to who was going to live in the model village.

Mr. Quaidoo explained. "You see, Papayebre was conceived as a project to incorporate several villages into a large town which can support the cost and upkeep of a sewage system, light, plumbing, paving, and all the other modern conveniences."

"Which are the lucky villages?" I asked.

Mr. Quaidoo flung his arm in three different directions. "The overflow of the inhabitants of Gyaamen, Abesiva, and Japa will be the first to move in, and as it increases in scope we hope to include other surrounding villages. However, one of the purposes in setting up a model village like this is to provide a showplace so that people from all over Ghana can come and study it and build similar towns of their own."

My conversational obsession of the summer was to steer all talk in the direction of Crossroads. "What is the building the Crossroaders are working on?" I asked.

Mr. Quaidoo said, "That is the Community Center. It is to be a combination of a town hall and a recreation center. Incorporated in the Community Center is a large office which is to be used in the first instance as a temporary clinic under the jurisdiction of Mrs. Mills, who at the moment is the nurse in charge of the clinic at Acrapong. Mrs. Mills and her husband live here in my house, and she will be able to visit the Papayebre clinic once or twice a week to give treatment for minor ailments. Eventually, as the village grows, I hope we will be able to build a permanent clinic. There is another office at the Community Center that we plan to use as a temporary post office until we can erect a permanent building of this nature. The Crossroaders will only be able to finish one section of it this summer, but we hope to have the rest completed in time for the Christmas celebrations."

I asked if there had been the usual trouble with supplies that most of the other Crossroad groups had experienced.

"We did run into a snag with the cement blocks. The villagers did not take care in protecting the Russian cement from the dampness when it was delivered at the work site, and it is taking about two weeks for the blocks to dry out. The Africans and Crossroaders could manufacture blocks in great numbers in our block-making machine, but they would not be ready for use on the project for a long time."

"I should think this would have delayed the work a great deal," I said.

"That's just what I feared. I found a solution, though. A church in town had a spare supply of blocks. I made an arrangement with them to exchange their dry blocks for our wet ones. It is a bit of a transportation problem; each villager is assigned twelve blocks a day to carry from the church to the work site. You will see a great procession of women and children, all coming to the project early tomorrow morning, carrying blocks on their heads."

"Who are the Africans working on the project?" I asked.

"We have six masons and two carpenters employed by the government. The rest are townspeople. They are farmers who all give up three days a week to share in this communal labor."

"How has the work been divided between the Africans and Crossroaders?"

"The African workers are divided in different groups, and the Crossroaders are assigned to each of these teams. Each crew is assigned a different job each day, and once a week we have meetings to discuss any problems. It has worked out very well this way."

"Who made the plans for the model village?"

"It was designed by the Town Planning Department of the Western Region. However we have benefited greatly from the advice of Garwood-Jones. It was lucky for us that the Crossroaders brought an architect with them." (Trevor Garwood-Jones, a Crossroader, is an architect from Hamilton, Ontario.) "He has replanned the Community Center the Crossroaders are working on so that it takes much better advantage of the site, improves the cross ventilation, and generally enhances the appearance of the building. The District Building Inspector was very pleased with the new design. Your architect has also been of great help to our masons, giving them special instruction in building."

As we left the edge of the balcony to return to our seats among the other Crossroaders and members of his household, I asked Mr. Quaidoo if there had been much of a language problem between the Crossroaders and the villagers, as I had heard that only the educated Africans spoke English in Gyaamen.

"Conversations have had their limitations," he said, "but they exchange so much in gestures and smiles. Every Saturday night the village of Gyaamen arrives with its own brass band for a dance. They have taught all the Crossroaders how to dance high life. In the afternoon they have volley ball games. They started with soccer, but that is our national sport, and the Crossroaders just couldn't keep up with the Africans."

Tony Blackburn joined the conversation by explaining to me that, although none of the desired students had been assigned to this project, three Mass Education workers who were living with them had provided the type of more intellectual contact the Crossroaders were looking for.

Mr. Quaidoo said, "The Mass Education program is to promote reading and writing among the adults who have never had a chance at an education. The Crossroaders have been able to give them a lot of help."

Tony added, "Also we have the teachers to talk to. We live in one of the four school buildings. School is in session now, and every day children have classes in the other three buildings of our quadrangle. We have all gotten to know these children, and most of the Crossroaders have taken over some of the classes when they weren't working on the project. Everyone has something different to offer. It's been an asset having so many professional people in our group."

As we got up to leave, Mr. Quaidoo winked. "You can see why I want to get that law of mine passed."

As we walked through the courtyard, Mr. Quaidoo took me off to one side and whispered, "Let me tell you a secret to show you how much the Crossroaders have meant to my people this summer. You know, they are very poor people. Well, they are collecting all their little gold possessions and melting them so that the village jeweler can make parting gifts for each Crossroader out of the collected gold. They call it their 'widow's mite.' I think they have planned gold necklaces for the five girls with a pendant inscribed with the word 'love' on each. The ten boys are going to receive gold lapel pins consisting of a moon and star, symbolizing the eternity of their friendship and memory in Papayebre." When he told me this there was an emotion in his voice that hadn't been there when he was talking about the progress of the building.

As we walked down the hill from Mr. Quaidoo's house that night, there was one question that was bothering me. Was it true that this extraordinary statesman and imaginative philanthropist had been forced to resign as Minister of the Interior?

The rumor I had heard was correct; Mr. Quaidoo had been

dismissed as Minister of the Interior two months ago. This was very hard to understand, and no one could give the exact reasons. One of the Crossroaders slipped me a clue in the form of a pamphlet giving the address delivered by Mr. Quaidoo, Minister of the Interior, during the Parliamentary Debates before the National Assembly on Tuesday, April 25, 1961. It said, in part:

Since the 8th of April, 1961, whether by design or accident, the prestige of Parliament has been made to descend rather low, and at this time it behooves every member of Parliament to uphold the authority of Parliament. God will never come down and fight for us. We must fight ourselves. . . .

We can talk, but I feel sure that we can do more than that. We do not just sit here and talk. We have the power to approve and disapprove; that is the sovereign right which every citizen of Ghana must recognize. Every institution of high supremacy must recognize parliamentary authority. Parliamentary sovereignty is not confined to Members of Parliament alone, but to everybody within the territorial boundaries of Ghana. . . .

And then some people, in order to win favor, instead of speaking boldly—after all it is our fine criticisms and fine suggestions that can help the leader to build the country—they do not do so. I think this is a very dangerous tendency, and it is like a canker worm which is spreading through the social fabric of this country. It is this which is dangerous. Instead of people speaking out their minds and saying the pros and cons about what should be done and giving advice, they keep silent and would rather want to know what the leader would like to hear. . . . Originality is what we need; it does not matter whether what we say is adopted or not, but we have a sacred duty to talk. . . .

The next thing we have is regard for proper procedure. If you go through our institutions, say chieftaincy or the way we do everything, our people have proper respect for procedure and they have to adopt procedural propriety in order to effect innovation. But the new teachers are telling us to put this aside.

Perhaps the most important is the sanctity of our family life. There are very few communities in this world who have family relationships as wide as ours. And I think it is unfortunate for us that the European system should have been adopted. With us we have a very big circle, and the practicing of charity to our fellow men is so easy because it is ingrained in our society. With us it is not man, wife, and child forming a unit; it is a very big circle, and our social life itself makes it possible to show charity to those who may be in difficulties and to observe the law, "Love thy neighbor as thyself." Whenever there is an attempt, however covert, on the sanctity of family life, let us realize that our whole foundation is being uprooted. These things are very insidious. . . .

I now address myself to expose some of the techniques being used to hoodwink us all into acquiescence. The methods which are being used are exactly the methods which the Nazis and Fascists used. The pity of it all is that what they are doing is most unsuited to the circumstances.

It is only when you have your leadership imposed upon you from above—if, for instance, you have a leader coming out of a military coup, then you have to have all those unnecessary trappings to uphold authority. But in Ghana, Osagyefo [Nkrumah] came from below—there is such a broad base. He is one of us, but the people want him to be among us and yet not one of us. That is what we members of Parliament must kick against. . . .

Now, Sir, in his speech, the President referred to intellectual freedom. Those who fought for independence fought in the hope that there would be true intellectual freedom. The story I cited of the teacher who told his pupils they should not ask any questions is a clear sign of intellectual enslavement, and, if carried out on a large scale, we are all to be spectators of a drama in Ghana— tragic comedy.

So if we are to build a society that is going to make use of all available resources in Ghana, then we must cast aside all these ideas of Leninism and Marxism and come down to Ghana to build on our own culture and that of Africa; because there is far more in our society and culture than Karl Marx or Lenin or anybody could have possibly thought of. At least we should not be copying machines. So I am only appealing that those who serve as teachers must first of all serve a term of apprenticeship and have the intellectual honesty which must characterize every scholar.

Mr. Speaker, I think I have sufficiently exposed some of those things which are going to undermine us so as to enable this House to take a firm decision as to how best we can preserve the integrity of Ghana by asserting its parliamentary supremacy.

(*Ghana Parliamentary Debates, Official Report, National Assembly, Tuesday, 25 April, 1961. Vol. 23, no. 6, pp. 166-180.*)

These were congenial thoughts to an American. We tend to embrace every semblance of our democracy wherever it appears. The very strength of our conviction that our form of democracy is innately true and right makes it difficult for us to accept any variation of the familiar. Sometimes we don't even realize how ingrained are our beliefs until we see them seriously challenged. One of the hardest adjustments for Crossroaders or any other American living abroad is the realization that what works best at home is not necessarily the answer for people in other parts of the world.

Early in October 1961, I picked up the *New York Times* to read that Mr. P. K. K. Quaidoo and forty-eight other Ghanians had been arrested and imprisoned (under the Preventive Detention Act) for their political beliefs. I felt as if not only an African but a little bit of America had been silenced behind the bars in Accra.

It was with great relief that I heard that on May 5, 1962, President Nkrumah announced the immediate release of many of those political prisoners. Fortunately Mr. Quaidoo was among those released.

This is the unfinished story of Mr. Quaidoo and his dream village of Papayebre. The Community Center, started by the

Crossroaders, was finished in time for Christmas. Mr. Trevor Garwood-Jones writes me from Canada that he is working on the architectural plans for the residential section of Papayebre.

Maybe the handwriting was on the wall when the name of the village was chosen. *Papayebre* translated from the Twi tongue means "It is difficult doing good all the time."

11

Mali

THE WORK PROJECT WAS ONLY PART OF THE CROSSROADS SUMMER plan. Almost equally important was the time set aside for travel, for it gave the dimension in breadth to the depth experience of the work camp. Those who had worked in the bush had a chance to see life in the cities and talk to more influential people. Those who had experienced the stimulation of the city had the chance to ob- serve African life in the bush. It was the time to see the "sights."

The Kenya group went water-skiing between hippopotami in Uganda and were entertained by Haile Selassie in Ethiopia. The Rhodesia group visited Victoria Falls and the Kariba Dam. The Gabon group visited Albert Schweitzer at his hospital in Lam- barene. Every group visited at least one other country besides the one they lived and worked in. The Crossroaders who worked on a school in Popenguine, a fishing village in Senegal, were one of the few groups to have their travel time before their work period.

Tommy Holahan, a Yale student from Long Island, was a member of the Senegal group. He was a relaxed, jolly person with a sandy complexion. I asked him how he happened to come to Af- rica with Crossroads.

Tommy said he'd heard about it from Kathy Rogers. "She was pushing Crossroads, and the thing that excited me most about her description of her summer with Bill Coffin's group in Guinea was the fun that she had just working casually on the job at Mamou. My past eight summers have been spent sailing or teaching sailing in Madison, Connecticut, where there was a great spirit and fun invoked among the sailing crowd by working together on the boats and then sailing them. Although I had been vaguely interested in Africa and current affairs, this chance for an experience of spirit, fun, and casual cooperation within a group performing manual labor was the biggest attraction of Crossroads." Tommy took jobs during Christmas, spring, and June vacations to supplement gifts from the Rotary, Lions, and Kiwanis service clubs, two high-school clubs, family, and friends, to pay for his trip.

He has been kind enough to share his summer's journal, which is as masculine in observation as Cathy Cobb's is feminine. Here are his impressions of their travels from Senegal to Mali before settling down in Popenguine.

Dakar, Senegal: Our major impressions so far have been those of tremendous contrasts between wild barren land and well-paved, well-curved roads; the beautiful clean buildings of Dakar center and its suburbs, and the incredibly poor, filthy and hopeless shacks of shanty sections; the Western clothes of the students and the French and the beautiful African dresses and the robes of the Moslem men; and the beauty of the African faces and the ugliness of disease.

Kayar, Senegal: Wednesday we visited the fishing village of Kayar, thirty miles north of Dakar. Here we got a wonderful capsule view of a funny interaction of old tradition and very new, modern Western ideas. The rhythm of the village is controlled by the coming and the going of the fishes. During slack seasons whole sections of the thatched villages crumble, to be rebuilt when fishing is good again; village shopkeepers come and go according to the same rhythm. The natives go out across the surf in their decorated dugout boats, some powered by Evinrude motors, and fill them with fish which they bring back and dry in big, fly-infested piles on the sand. Because the village is such an important fish center, the government has built a modern storage warehouse with good drying racks, in hopes of improving the quality of the export. The natives, of course, keep drying their fish on the beach and use the racks for drying their clothes.

Bamako, Mali: Bamako is alive with diplomats, shady intrigues from all sides, and political maneuvering. The eastern block is making a big play for Mali ever since she split off from the Federation of Senegal, which was a mis-match from the first. The links between Mali and Guinea are very strong and I believe a rail line is being built from Bamako to the sea via Conakry to replace the Bamako-Dakar line which has been severed by the sealing off of the Mali-Senegal border. Bamako needs 100 tons of fuel every day, and this takes 15 big twenty-ton trucks coming 500 miles daily from Abidjan. Mali has really cut its nose off by refusing to open the frontier to Senegal.

Mali's big problem is this year's peanut crop. Peanuts are 90 per cent of their export and worth ten million dollars. France offered to buy peanuts right off the farms at 105 francs per kilogram. To prove their economic independence, Mali decided to sell to the eastern bloc. The deal was 105 francs per kilogram, but at shipside (whereas France paid 105 francs at the fields), so Mali had to arrange to pay for transport. The 1000 privately owned trucks in the area smelled trouble, and only 178 showed up. The result is that much of the crop has been lying useless in the rain with the value dropping. Furthermore, Russia will only pay 50 per cent in currency and the other 50 per cent in Russian goods.

We visited the American Embassy. I was impressed by the American ambassador and how hardheaded and at the same time how sympathetic he was—and what a good understanding he had of the aims of Crossroads.

Thursday night we were invited to attend a rally, sponsored by the Youth Party to demonstrate the solidarity between the youth of Mali and Algeria. Forewarned of the theme, we were surprised to see the rally hall plastered with large photographs of fat pigs, hefty cattle, and plump peasants, all showing the inflated economic prosperity of the People's Republic of Mongolia. The Chinese and Mongolian ambassadors were given seats of honor. There were about 400 Africans between the ages of eighteen and thirty. We were the only Americans. After a one-and-a-half-hour wait, Mali's president, Modibo Kieta, a tall proud giant of a man dressed in his white flowing African robe, arrived to give the rally the approval of his presence. There were three short speeches: the head of the Youth Party outlined the history of the seven-year-old revolution in Algeria; the secretary of the Mali National Labor Union and the Algerian ambassador to Mali both emphasized their dislike of colonial domination and their prophecies (greeted by cheers) of its early downfall. We wandered out of the hall in time to see Modibo Kieta's motorcycle-escort bomb off in the wrong direction, leaving the president stranded. The resulting chaos was fun, but distressingly typical.

Kayes, Mali: Our travels covered a great part of the breadth of Mali, and each city has something different and outstanding to offer. Kayes is a center for peanuts and hydroelectricity on the Senegal River, and, with the rail line cut to Senegal, it is the last stop for the Mali railroad. There we saw the large road toward Guinea which will solve Mali's problem of access to the sea. The roadbed is being laid by the voluntary work of all the citizens, which the Malians call l'investment humaine—human investment program.

Except during the summer harvest and crop months, the political party (which sponsors the work with only tools and materials from the government) manages to have 5000 citizens at work on the road. The work is progressing at 800 meters a day. It's an amazing accomplishment, because the project is not a forced one; it springs from the devotion of the Malians and the desire to build their country.

Ségou, Mali (on the other side of Bamako): We saw a project

started in 1938 by the French. This was the Niger project, a large dam across the Niger River and a series of canals used to irrigate a large stretch of land for rice and cotton—land that was formerly arid and unpopulated. Now it is the most highly populated region of Mali, and the project is shared by the Mali government. Talking to our guide, a young Malian teacher, I tried to use the Niger project as an example of how French colonialism had been beneficial to the Malians; but he quickly pointed out that the original French designs were to use the project as a cotton center, which would be useless to Mali. Well, what can you say?

Mopti, Mali: Mopti is sort of the middle of the lake country of Mali. Built on two islands, the country around has been reclaimed for rice cultivation by dikes. During the rainy season the land is inundated and the rice is harvested by boat. Mopti is the beginning of the area which encompasses superstitious remnants of old Malian pagan tribes. The founding of the city is woven into a legend about a Moroccan who comes and signs a pact with a water sprite, to which the descendants of the original Moroccan sacrifice a lamb every year.

Bandiagara and Sangha, Mali: We drove from Mopti along a treacherous, rocky path of a road into the mountainous region of Mali. In Bandiagara we saw three châteaux of several stories, built in mud by ancient kings. We drove on to Sangha, a well-known Dogon village. The Dogons are one of the oldest tribes and cliff dwellers of Mali. They originally built their stone villages on the tops of craggy hills, surrounding them with rocky walls to blend in with the countryside and protect them against hostile attacks from foreign tribes. They continue their ancient way of life, even to the extent of carrying baskets of soil from the valleys six kilometers away to make artificial fields for their millet. We saw many such hand-made fields with whole families working in them. They are deeply superstitious people and still go through the old mask dances and fetish-worshiping ceremonies. We were received by the Chief of Sanghi, who led us down through the millet fields to another village built over a natural limestone cave about 100 yards

long. Through the tunnel we came upon the edge of a large valley and were able to look down on two more Dogon villages built
right under the face of the cliff. Beyond in the setting sunlight lay
a vast plain stretching all the way to the Upper Volta.

One of the most exciting aspects of our trip to various parts
of Mali is the way our receptions have been organized. We have
been in the hands of the Bureau of Youth and Sports, a part of
the government which has a branch in every city and village.
Through these local branches our food, lodging, and program of
activities are arranged. At every place our program has included
réunion avec les jeunesse, where we get a chance to ask questions
about Mali and answer questions about the U.S.A. There are two
major questions which the Africans keep bringing up. One is on
their neutrality; the other is on our racism.

The Mali youth feel that America's stand in the Cold War
against Russia has tainted her African policy. They dislike having
America worry about whether they will be going communist or
not. They feel that America has sided with the colonial powers of
England, France, and Portugal who have falsely used communism
to explain the new forces working in Africa. They openly state
that such anxiety is an insult to their own political competence
and maturity.

The Mali Youth questioned how it was possible for America
to work for world peace with the very unpeaceful segregation problem yet unsolved at home. They do not understand how the law
of the federal government can be by-passed by the state and local
governments. They were less interested in hearing about the progress being made than in stressing that segregation must be eradi-
cated immediately, that Africa as a growing third force in the
world can accept nothing less. They are convinced that segregation is one of the major reasons why America will fail to achieve
totally friendly relations in the black nations of the world.

Although Tom had spent eight summers sailing off Madison,
Connecticut, it was something else again to determine which way

the wind was blowing and who had the right of way in a country like Mali. But, as Tommy Holahan said, "You have to go with it —nice and easy—feel your way." Like pointing a small boat up into the wind.

12

Guinea

THE CROSSROADERS WERE THE GUESTS OF SEVENTEEN VERY DIFFER-
ent African countries. Some of the host countries were in a position to give more all-out attention than the guests could absorb.
In Sierra Leone the Crossroaders were so strenuously entertained
that they were sometimes too exhausted for the work project.
Other countries were so concerned with their own busy lives that
they left the guests to fend for themselves. Guinea had a very hectic household, due to the turbulent conditions under which she
had acquired her independence. The Crossroaders were not seeking entertainment, but they wanted desperately to get out back
and help with the work to be done. They were left waiting at the
door for four weeks. It was never quite clear whether Guinea was
too preoccupied with the organization of its household to let the
Crossroaders in, or whether she was trying to get rid of the guests
as unobtrusively as possible.

Guinea was also suffering from a history of disturbed emotional relationships with outsiders. The Guineans were aware that
the United States was a friend of France, and they had no reason
to believe that the friend of the parent would behave any differ-

ently from the parent. The Crossroaders were in a position to inherit some of the bitter and suspicious attitudes stimulated by the relationships of the past.

Guinea had belonged to a large African family of twelve. In 1958, when de Gaulle took over the French household, he sensed that all the African offspring were edging toward independence. This gave him a feeling of uneasiness, and he asked for a vote of confidence from all the African countries, inviting them to join a new association with France. Eleven responded, *"Oui, oui."* Guinea was the twelfth, and she had no intention of compromising with independence. For Guinea it was all or nothing. The answer to de Gaulle's question was definitely *"Non!"*

Guinea realized that the cord she was cutting involved financial aid as well as assured trade. In his now famous proclamation, Sékou Touré said, "We would rather have freedom in poverty than riches in slavery."

France could not tolerate this kind of insulting talk, and was determined to punish rude Guinea as a lesson to the eleven others. Anyone who chose not to communicate with home should be discouraged from all other communications. So the departing French staff removed all the telephones in Conakry; they took the telephone wiring, the directories, and the operators; they removed desks, files, maps, and records. The defiant should be left defenseless. The French removed all the guns, the ammunition, and the soldiers' uniforms. Those who ignore parental teaching should not have access to any learning; all but a handful of French school teachers evacuated Guinea. The unenlightened should be left in the dark; when the French left Conakry they removed electric light bulbs. The lesson should be clear to the other eleven countries that there was only one safe way to independence—the parental way! By the time the French departed from Conakry with their loot, the Guineans were ready to rid themselves of the last vestiges of the parental image. They took all the statues of French heroes, which had been elegantly dominating the neat squares of Conakry, from their pedestals, and lined them up on the shore with their backs to Guinea, facing out to sea and toward France.

This parental showdown precipitated Guinea's independence earlier than she had anticipated. In her forsaken state, Guinea turned to the United States for help. Unfortunately the United States was having a little difficulty with the new head of the French household. It seemed more strategic to secure relationship with the parent than to risk association with this newcomer. Rejected by the United States, Guinea in economic desperation turned to Ghana, which threw out the first lifeline in the form of a considerable loan. Guinea appealed to Senegal for teachers, and teachers were sent. Guinea then turned to Russia and her friends. The Eastern bloc were glad to communicate with Guinea and were quick to offer loans and trade agreements. France and the United States having become anxious as they realized that Guinea had turned to these dubious strangers, both approached Guinea with some second-thought propositions. Bankrupt Guinea decided on neutrality as the safest role for a country struggling to establish its independence.

The Crossroaders did not anticipate what it would be like getting to know this country. They had hoped to go straight from Conakry to Mamou to finish the youth hostel that last year's group had started; this had been the earlier understanding. But when they arrived in Conakry they were taken right down to the Ministry of Youth and Sports to discuss the arrangements of their program, and the Minister suggested that the Crossroaders take a two-week tour of the country while the Ministry of Youth consider the plan for their working at Mamou. The Crossroaders left on the suggested trip, spent two weeks seeing the major centers of Guinea, and returned, on July 17, to Conakry with crossed fingers in anticipation of the work project.

Willard Johnson, the Crossroads leader, went down to the Ministry of Youth and Sports to make arrangements. The Minister reported that they had made no preparations for the Crossroaders to work on the project. The following day, July 18, Willard returned to the Ministry but did not succeed in talking to anyone except for brief hello's in the corridor. On July 19, Willard went down to the Ministry of Youth and Sports, exchanged more hello's in the corridor, and was asked to come back the following day.

As Willard went "home" to the expectant Crossroaders each day, repeating the same weary message of frustration, he began to feel like a stuck phonograph needle unable to move on to the anticipated melody.

One Crossroader said, "I don't think they want us."

Another Crossroader said, "If they're going to claim they're neutral, they can't reject us. There are no other voluntary American groups to be neutral with in Guinea."

Willard said, "It really is hard to know whether they're giving us the cold shoulder or are bogged down by administrative difficulties. After all, they did have to start from scratch when the French walked out."

Another Crossroader said, "We've got to convince them we're not here to kid around, but that we really want to work and help them."

Willard sighed. "Well, I'll try again tomorrow."

Finally, on July 20, Willard succeeded in seeing the Minister of Youth, who reported that the youth hostel at Mamou didn't fit in with Guinea's "three-year plan" and they weren't at all sure they could supply the necessary materials. Willard explained that the Crossroaders didn't care where they worked, but they did want to start doing something useful. The Minister asked Willard to come and see him "tomorrow."

On July 21, Willard returned to the Ministry of Youth and Sports. The Minister said that he wanted Crossroads to draft plans for a little building with one room, veranda, and overhanging roof, about seven by nine meters, which could be built on the premises of the Ministry. This was to be a clubroom for little children. It sounded like a perfect Crossroads project.

Willard went running back to the Crossroaders to share the good news. They were overjoyed at the prospects, and all week end they worked night and day designing "the most beautiful little square building in the world."

On Monday, July 24, Willard proudly presented the plans to the Minister of Youth and Sports. About ten minutes later word came back that the Minister did not feel that the Crossroaders could finish the building in the time they had left. He suggested an alternative project, which was to clear off an overgrown and uncompleted tennis court located at the rear of the Ministry grounds. The Crossroaders were asked to expand the paved surface and mark it off. Willard expressed great disappointment that the other project had been brushed aside, but said that they would do anything they were asked to do.

Willard returned to a very discouraged group of Crossroaders. They had a momentous meeting that afternoon. Some felt it was time to quit.

One Crossroader remarked, "They're completely brushing us aside on a project of no significance to Guinea."

Another said, "It's located in such an out-of-the-way place, we're practically hidden from the Africans we'd like to contact."

"Let's go to Ghana," one of them suggested. "They've requested another Crossroads team there."

Other Crossroaders reminded the protesters that they were guests in Guinea and should follow through with anything they were asked to do.

One Crossroader was particularly upset because his entire trip had been financed by three thousand members of his home church.

"I refuse to go home and tell them that the only thing I did all summer was to weed a tennis court!" he said.

In anger the Crossroaders cleared the entire tennis court of waist-high weeds, in one day, to demonstrate to the Guineans that they were there to work.

Willard went back again to the Ministry of Youth and Sports that same afternoon to relay the feelings of the group. He reported that some of the Crossroaders had thought of going to

Ghana, where an additional team had been requested, but that they didn't really want to do that. They had chosen Guinea, liked it, and felt that it was important to learn as much as possible of Guinea's efforts, because they regarded Guinea as the model for much of the rest of Africa. Willard went on to say, "These young people have brought unlimited good will, a rare willingness, even eagerness to share completely the aspirations of the Guinean young people and their efforts to secure their own future."

Willard suggested that the project should be of such a nature that in itself it would symbolize the efforts of the Guinean youth to build and develop their country.

"Even in the United States," he said, "we consider a tennis court a luxury—a non-essential. I cannot imagine that the tennis court could be very high on the list of priorities for Guinea."

The Minister seemed straightforward and understanding. He replied, "*C'est juste*"—"You are entirely right." He agreed that the tennis court was not high on the priority list and that was the one reason it had been left unfinished. He confessed that the Ministry had been very embarrassed that they were not "ready" for the Crossroaders.

Willard mentioned that he had never fully understood why the Crossroaders had not been allowed to return to Mamou and continue the project started by last year's Crossroaders. Willard was asked to return the next day.

On Tuesday, July 25, Willard came back and was told that the Minister had decided to allow the Crossroaders to return to Mamou.

When Willard told the Crossroaders that they were going to Mamou, morale skyrocketed. They arrived at Mamou to find that the youth hostel had been almost finished by the 1960 Crossroads group. In the time that was left they were able to complete all but the laying on of the roof.

Although the Crossroaders had spent a frustrating four weeks waiting for their assignment, they felt that what they had learned about Guinea made it more than worth while. Guinea had been the one member of the French community that had believed so strongly in the principles of independence that she had had the courage to make the break with the parent country. She had cut off security for an ideal. It was this sense of self-direction that most impressed the Crossroaders. For Guinea, independence was not just a new President, a new flag, and a new constitution. Every Guinean shared a sense of pride and dedication to making their independence work. Guinea had become independent the rough, hard way, but the spirit which resulted gave independence a new look in Africa.

It was not easy to evaluate this rather hectic Crossroads experience at the time. Many Crossroaders have expressed the feeling that the real impact of their Crossroads summer catches up with them much later. Several months later, Andrea Cousins, a Sarah Lawrence girl spending her junior year abroad, wrote from Paris with fresh perspective:

20 November, 1961
Paris

Dear Mrs. Plimpton,

I'm glad you asked me about Guinea. Since I have been in Paris I've had some time/space for better digesting the summer. It's interesting to see once-French Africa from here, particularly Guinea. When an African statesman arrives in Paris all the flags go up, the traffic tangles, and there are honors all around throughout the day. That is to say those statesmen of the French community; I'm not quite sure how Guinea/Mali would fare under the same circumstances. One of the Guinean students admitted that it was unusually hard for him to get a job, yet the situation is not clear—other Guineans and Malians I've met seem at ease and happy with their life here. In any event one can see the deep wrenching away that Guinean independence involved—the French way of life is socially persuasive; the worship of la mode, the delight in good food, the casualness of the café, the life on the big boulevards—attractive shops, good theater, art galleries—all tanta-

lize the tourist, and those Africans who come for a few years are probably no exception. Among the French one has the impression that there is nothing much better than being French-cultured, and despite the skepticism of all things political there's the assumption that this civilization is a nice one to be attached to. During the past three months I've more and more come to respect the signifi-cance of Guinea's decision, the rather awesome courage which it represents. I've also been gaining a deeper appreciation for the character of the people (the Guineans) themselves; perhaps it is Parisian, perhaps it is merely the bigness of the city, but one feels here little rapport with the people who swarm the streets. In light of the detached curiosity which marks the Frenchman's regard for anyone not of his ilk, the Guineans' warmth and interest in a band of partly white, Western (and American) students appears to me more and more gratifying.

I remember walking up from the work project through the main street of Mamou—how voices would call out to us by name, how the children would run after us, how the shopkeepers would smile—"Ça va?" When the French landlady complains about her hot-water supply, about her electricity costs, about the door only half-bolted, I think of our walking into a dimly lit hut, the dis-tance a villager would go to bring us some pineapple juice, the trouble we had carrying the ears of corn and the live chickens which were given us as we left. There is a longing in me to be again on African Standard Time—time set to the rhythm of your hands, of your appetite, of the sun. I like to think of people's faces as they danced the cha-cha-cha, or as they took our hands into a circle for the kabindo. There were so few physical props used for social entertainment—they had their voices, their hands, their humor and fantasy. The girls would teach us intricate games that involved imaginative clapping and singing patterns. The boys would show us how to find a grapefruit tree, or how to knock down a coconut. Their bodies were hard and graceful. We learned to reap ladders and scaffolding from a grove of saplings, how it is possible to mix cement on the floor without a tub or a wheelbar-

row. . . . *The sense of community pervaded almost any situation:
one truck breaks down and everyone in a mile radius comes to
clear another roadway; a tree stands dead at the side of a street,
and twenty men join in the felling of it.*

*The spirit carries over naturally into politics. Base committees
organized throughout the forty-three sections of the country provide a structure "founded," in the words of Sékou Touré, "on the
will and interest of the people." Being a Guinean means deep in-
volvement in the state of the nation. It means giving one day of
the week to a community work project—the building of a road,
a maternity clinic, a classroom. It means participation in the
Youth Movement (JRDA) if you're under thirty and over eight
years of age, in the union movement if you're in a trade (and even
the women are organized). Ask a Guinean how his life has
changed since the country's independence—he might answer, as
one boy answered me, with the gentle reply, "On se sent a l'aise
. . . on se sent libre." At ease and free. This means the willingness
to spend yourself at the demands of your own destiny, it means
working for something which would fall without you or triumph
in your name. It is this vital relation of the individual to the community—and in Guinea this community begins in Dalaba, or
Mamou, or Kankan, and extends to the entité humaine—which
draws me back to this corner of Africa, with the hope of becom-
ing a necessary part.*

*I hope this letter helps you, Mrs. Plimpton—it has certainly
helped me. Thank you, I was needing to put it into words.*

Sincerely,

Andrea

P. S. *Give my love—please—to Willard. I keep missing him.*

13

Black and White

As WILLARD ENTERED THE HOTEL DE FRANCE IN CONAKRY, ANDREA turned to me and said, "We're so proud of our leader—not just because he's an expert political scientist and has taught us so much about Guinea, but more because we love the way he walks in a room. We know that he knows that he's just as good as any white man present, if not better." Willard was an inspiring leader for the Guinea group because he exemplified a Negro who had suffered the indignities and discouragements of growing up in the segregated South, and yet he had managed to discover and assert his own human worth.

For many Crossroaders the summer offered the first opportunity for Negro and white students to meet as individuals rather than representatives of different races. One girl confessed that her first reaction on being introduced to her group in Washington was to make a careful count of "how many blacks and how many whites" there were.

"By the end of the summer," she said, "I couldn't have told you. I was too busy counting something else—the number of good friends I'd made—and color had nothing to do with it."

The group experience held different meanings for Crossroaders from different parts of the country. Cathy Cobb's letter expresses the attitude shared by many Crossroaders from the Middle West and Canada. They had read about racial problems in the newspapers, but they had never had a first-hand introduction before.

The Negro and white Crossroaders from the South had grown up in segregated circles. For many of them, Crossroads offered a first opportunity to meet as equals. Julius Coles had known only the Negro population of Atlanta, Georgia. Every single student at Morehouse College had contributed one dollar toward sending him on Crossroads. Since his return, his Crossroad speeches have served to bring him in contact with many white people in Atlanta, and several of his white Crossroads friends have been to visit him. For him the Crossroads experience was a barrier-breaker.

White Crossroaders from the North had their eyes opened not only to the conspicuous problems of segregation in the South, but the rather inconspicuous instances of integration in the North. They could no longer point to one Negro in one college fraternity and pretend that all racial problems were centered in the South.

For some Crossroaders it was the first chance to air feelings of race resentment which had been pocketed away for many years. It was the intimate exposure in daily living together which encouraged them to express many of the feelings which are so easily inhibited in the hustle and bustle of ordinary life. The honest exchange of grudges served to dissipate the very attitudes they expressed.

"Don't you discuss race relations the same way in your bull sessions at college?" I asked a group of Negro and white students who were attending the same college.

"Not the same wholehearted way," one of them said. "We usually have an approaching exam or some other distraction on our minds."

It was the interaction of honest emotions expressed by such different types of Crossroaders that made the group experience so meaningful. Many Crossroaders expressed their reluctance to write home because their thoughts were too profound to risk communicating to those so far away.

Crossroaders were striving for a proximity of spirits on such a deep level that it was going to seem like turning the clock back to return to the issues of segregation in schools, buses, restaurants, etc., in the United States. Some white Crossroaders were realizing that in their great desire to compensate for the hurts of segregation they had swung over too far in the supportive direction. Therefore they were trying to establish relationships in which white Crossroaders felt free to treat their Negro friends in the same casual and sometimes blunt manner that they expressed toward their white friends, without being emotionally "on guard," for the "guards" were the greatest inhibitors of spontaneous friendships. It would be almost humanly impossible for a Negro who had experienced the insults of our society today not to be a little supersensitive. The white Crossroaders, in their lighthearted way, could do a lot to help their Negro friends find a balance between fact and fancy.

Crossroaders could no longer regard the problems of race relationships as a vague cause. Every Crossroader had become personally involved. They had become black and white partners working together for a shared ideal. Race relationships will never be solved by black people agitating alone for their rights which infringe on the rights of white people. Integration can only come about through intelligent black and white people working in unison, with understanding of the human strengths and frailties on both sides. Neither guilt nor revenge is a happy motive. What Crossroaders learned was how much black and white people have to give one another, once they have the opportunity.

Much of the time the Negro Crossroaders served as passports to Africa for the white Crossroaders. The Negroes often received slightly preferential treatment from the Africans. The suspicious Africans were lured by the fact that these Negroes found the white

Americans fit companions. It was a healthy turn-about tale that it was an advantage to be an American Negro in Africa. Bernice Parr was invited to assist the midwife in Achina in the delivery of several Nigerian babies. Don Harris was chosen as the one eligible member of the Kitwe group to attend the Northern Rhodesian National Conference at Broken Hill. The other white Crossroaders turned quite green with envy. Don was the only American to attend the "closed sessions" and he dined and conversed with Kenneth Kaunda, president of the United National Independence Party. As a result of the contact, Kaunda later visited the Crossroaders in Kitwe. There are many African doors which are still closed to white Americans but for which the American Negro holds the "open sesame." Crossroads appreciates the asset of the Negro but has had great difficulty in recruiting sufficient numbers. Last year only 30 of the 220 Crossroaders were Negroes. Finances are a big obstacle, but attitude can be another deterrent.

The American Negro is, of course, finding his early heritage in Africa. It is a fallacy to assume that inheritance is more important than environment in this instance. The American Negro is *first* American—not African; it is a loyalty our country should work hard to deserve.

The "cultural shock" the American Negro experiences in Africa is not very different from that experienced by white Americans. But despite difficulties in this adjustment, it is not a foregone conclusion that "American Negroes and Africans do not like each other." That is very harmful propaganda at this trial period, and to judge from my observations last summer it simply is not true. Like everyone else, they need the opportunity to get to know each other under desirable circumstances.

The experience of going back to Africa is by no means uniform for all Negroes. Some find a natural fulfillment in the identity of their heritage. Fannie Byrd, a Crossroads leader in 1960, writes of how the Crossroads experience led her to return to her present job in Africa with the YWCA in Kampala, Uganda:

As a Negro, I felt for the first time a sense of really belonging: that Africa was the country where I had roots. The feeling of personal identity with Africans, which is one of the objectives of Crossroads—in a sociological sense—became a much more subjective experience for me. I wanted intensely to have a part in helping the Africans in their race against time to assume all the responsibilities and privileges of being free, independent citizens in a free and independent society of nations.

Other Negroes express reservations. Don Harris says:

The American Negro will never be able to identify or relate himself completely to the African. Not only will the African not allow it, but I feel it is impossible for the American, no matter how long the individual remains in Africa.

A black American will think, speak, and react first as an American. The culture gap is far too wide to bridge completely. Even though he may eventually accustom himself to bartering for a loaf of bread every day, tolerate the smells of the marketplace, and get used to "robots" and "roundabouts" and similar "inconveniences," he will never become an African: his logic wouldn't permit him to understand "Juju" (a form of West African mysticism) and his conscience wouldn't permit him to believe in some of the rituals.

Beyond all this, the African won't accept us, as Negroes, Americans, and foreigners, completely, because an American Negro in Africa is principally an American.

Whether his personal reaction is one of complete or incomplete identity, the American Negro can be a very important link with Africa, and should be given every encouragement and opportunity to serve in the Peace Corps, State Department, or any other foreign service.

Every Crossroader got a fresh look at his country from afar last summer. The one outstanding impression was that: unless the black and white people of the United States can create the kind of opportunities to know each other as individuals which the Cross-roaders experienced last summer, our great country will lose its last chance as a democratic image in the world today. No matter how much diplomatic lipstick we spread on, our exterior looks can be no more beautiful than what we are inside. No one is going to be impressed by our big world-brotherhood grin, in a two-thirds colored world, if it does not reflect an internal reality. Neither the men in the White House, our United Nations representatives, nor our emissaries abroad can control the American image. All the work of our best statesmen can be either undermined or enhanced by what goes on between black and white individuals at home. There is not a single American who cannot find the opportunity to improve race relationships in some small, if not big, way. One doesn't have to go to Africa "to do something constructive." The American image shines out from within.

14

Return

WHAT APPEARED TO BE A GREAT CONFUSION OF ARRIVALS AND DEPAR-
tures was simply routine at Idlewild. Of all the thousands of travelers swarming about the airport, there were two distinct categories
of people—Crossroaders and the others. After one glance there
was absolutely no question as to who was a Crossroader and who
was just "somebody else." They strolled off the airfield in groups
—"real casual" travelers. Some were in African attire and others
in simple American clothes, but everyone had something African
about him. They were carrying spears, tom-toms, and miniature
dugout canoes. Some lugged shields, carved heads, or wicker fishing traps. There were baskets, fetish dolls, and painted banana
leaves. When the customs officials opened their bulging bags, I
could see the smaller packable items: ivory elephants, ebony ga-
zelles, and little brass Africans at work—all souvenirs of the summer.

Robinson had warned them, "You may leave Africa, but Africa will never leave you." He was not referring to those colorful
purchases. The real African treasures were hidden from the customs officials, for they were smuggled in in the hearts and heads of

the Crossroaders. These were the intangible riches of Africa and they were duty-free at Idlewild—but not for long.

Every Crossroader was duty bound to share these experiences and to bring back as many African images as he could to those who had made his trip possible. Already some of the families were on the balcony overlooking the customs, pressing noses to the large expanse of glass and exchanging joyous glances of recognition as their Africanized offspring set foot on American soil once more. For some families it had taken real courage to allow their youngsters to participate in an adventure quite so unknown and strange to them. They were entering an exciting new stage of parenthood, which shifts its emphasis from teaching to learning. Then there were the hundreds of friends, schools, colleges, churches, and clubs which had shared in this African enterprise. They couldn't all go to Africa, so they had pinched pennies to send someone who would represent them in Africa and come back and tell them about it. Each Crossroader was someone's investment, and the dividends were the undeclared imports slipping past the X-ray eyes of the customs officials.

Most Crossroaders had farther to travel before they would be home. Doctor Robinson's associate, Mr. Lindsay H. White, had charge of all the "connections." A look at his list revealed flights in every possible direction from New York to near and far corners of the United States and Canada. Crossroaders would soon be spread across the country. Their contacts would not be limited to their circles of families, friends, and supporters. Each Crossroader had promised to give one talk a week for the following year. Their talks would reach beyond their local schools, churches, and clubs. They would also be addressing the larger audience of radio and television. They would be writing articles for newspapers and magazines. If you average the Crossroads audiences at one hundred people and take one big mathematical somersault, you get a figure close to one million, which would represent the number of Americans and Canadians who will hear something about Africa this year from these alert, attractive young citizens. It would be hard to imagine a more effective or refreshing educational device for introducing Africa to America.

The responsibility of giving these talks means continued learning, thinking, and articulating about Africa for the Crossroaders. As Tom Hoeber wrote from Wesleyan, "The speaking engagements we are committed to make here have taught me the art of public speaking as no course ever could have, and the constant stimulus has heightened my interest in Africa and continually made me aware of the complexity of it." Most Crossroaders have discovered that they are able to communicate some very important ideas to large numbers of people—a good way of discovering their own uniqueness. They know they aren't experts, but the future beckons.

Almost as important as the information which the Crossroaders could bring home were the facts and figures they had to leave in Africa. There was so much to learn and so much which could not yet be learned because of inadequate information. Africa is a haven of undiscovered mysteries. It had been a summer to stimulate curiosity. Every Crossroader had some special interest he or she wanted to pursue. Theirs had been a rare chance for relaxed observation in many fields—their minds were not yet preoccupied nor imaginations tightened by the responsibilities of an exacting job.

Important, too, was the fact that Crossroaders had been exposed to many fields of interest in many countries. A medical student in Togo had witnessed a case of witchcraft. He was intensely interested in learning how great the psychological gap is between such tribal beliefs and modern medicine. A law student in Abidjan had spent many hours with a judge whose job was to transfer the legal customs of the fifty-six tribes of the Ivory Coast to one workable legal code. Would prefabricated paper houses withstand the African climate and be acceptable to the people? Does a coffee bean have to cross the Atlantic twice before it lands in a coffee cup? Why are all the beautiful African cloths mostly printed in Holland and England? If African society became monogamous, how would an unmarried woman make out? There is no telling what may be the results when dedicated people with strong feelings make first-hand observations.

For many Crossroaders the summer experience would mean reshaping their studies, and for some, changing their careers. One of the greatest opportunities Crossroads had offered was the introduction to more permanent fields of service in Africa. The Crossroaders had been able to work with various members of the State Department, observe missionaries, and visit schools and hospitals. They had been introduced to American business abroad in mines, rubber plantations, and at Pepsi-Cola parties. Whatever their special interest or ability might be, this had been a summer to discover how they might fit the puzzling pieces of their lives into the overseas picture. It was as important for some to find they simply did not fit as for others to find the perfect answer to their dreams.

Each Crossroader had his or her individual gain from the summer's experience. It would be hard to predict their future.

Maybe the most telling indications would be the activities of their Crossroad predecessors. One-third of them had returned to Africa one way or another. There were six with the East African Teachers' Program and nine with the West African Teachers' Program. Seven were in the Ford Foundation Training Center, training to be civil servants in the Congo. Five were working in the State Department in Africa. Fourteen were working in African organizations. Thirteen were doing some sort of religious work. Many others were pursuing their graduate studies in the United States with African plans in mind.

For some Crossroaders the summer really was an introduction to Africa. Harry Qualman had never heard of Crossroads before he attended a banquet at Howard University in 1960. He had never been out of the United States before 1961, when he went to the Cameroons with Crossroads. He writes:

Before I went to Africa with Crossroads I had never considered studying Africa or specializing in it in any way. What made me change my mind? Well, during the course of the summer I think several things happened. First, I began to realize how wrong my original conceptions of Africa had been and how little I and other Americans knew about Africa. Second, I found Africa most challenging and enjoyed my summer there immensely. Third, all my experiences led me to realize what "underdeveloped" really means—and I came to realize how much more we had in America and how much development had yet to take place in Africa.

These three factors, plus the knowledge that there is a growing need for people who are "African experts," led me to a decision that I wanted to specialize in African studies. Therefore I applied for a Rotary Foundation Fellowship for International Understanding. I received this fellowship, and next year I will study African economic development at the University of Dakar, Senegal.

There were other Crossroaders who were already immersed in African studies and used the Crossroads summer as a testing ground to determine how seriously they wanted to pursue these studies. Yvonne Williams was with the 1960 Crossroads group in Togo. She tells how that experience influenced her in taking her present job as junior officer with USIS in Tunis, Tunisia.

My own interest and work on Africa pre-dates the Crossroads experience. I was engaged in research (at the undergraduate level) when I first heard of Crossroads. . . . For me, Crossroads provided the practical or realistic dimension to studies which had, up to that time, been limited to books and occasional social contacts with African students. Up to that time I had read about nationalism and underdevelopment, but these were merely words and concepts, rather than actual states of being which I myself could feel and experience. The Crossroads experience was the one that made me feel certain and confident that I wanted to specialize in the field of African affairs.

Shirley Barnes was one of the girls I met with the 1961 Togo group. I remember well a long conversation we had, perched on the end of our cots in that schoolroom. We were discussing the significance for a Negro in refinding his African heritage. I wondered at the time whether she was really serious about returning to Africa. My question was well answered by a letter received in April 1962.

At this time, I am in the Congo under the auspices of the Ford Foundation, working as Program Specialist. For me, coming back to Africa was the realization of a decision that I had made, even before going on Crossroads. Crossroads was the vehicle that launched me on my African experience. I had decided to try to come to Africa with Crossroads to see whether I really wanted to live here for any length of time. Without my having come on Crossroads, I would not be sitting here today writing you this letter.

Without a doubt, I believe that any person who has an interest in Africa, especially those students who would like someday to work in Africa, Crossroads is one of the most practical and rewarding ways to become acquainted with it. May I add that Crossroads is also a proving ground, for those who are not really made of the material needed for Africa at this time can be weeded out in the Crossroads experience.

Crossroads serves as a wonderful preparation for those who later join the Peace Corps. Twenty-seven Crossroaders have already joined the Peace Corps and forty more have signed up. The Recruitment Director of Peace Corps, Richard A. Grahame, asked Doctor Robinson for his entire list of former Crossroaders, because, as he wrote, "Certainly there could be no better training for Peace Corps Service than that provided by the experience with Operation Crossroads Africa." Letters from Crossroaders in the Peace Corps confirm this statement.

It is interesting that the most often repeated challenge to Crossroads is the person who says, "But don't you think that the greatest value of Crossroads is the experience it provides the individual Crossroader?" as if it were a disappointing accomplishment falling so far short of "saving all Africa." What greater success could one ask for than the heightening and enlightening of the individual? The most common reaction I have heard expressed by returning Crossroaders is, "This summer has completely changed my life." Even for the Crossroaders whose lives may lead in directions other than African affairs, the quality of their lives has been enhanced.

Many factors combine to make changes in people's lives. You can't put your finger on all of them. The impact of the continent of Africa had been tremendous, the group experience of living together unforgettable, but also the leadership of James H. Robinson had made a profound impression on many a Crossroader.

As one of them said, "Our families and friends think we're great just to go to Africa. They would let us rest on the status quo of a perfectly acceptable performance. Doctor Robinson never seems satisfied with us until we have stretched a little beyond what we thought was our very best."

I would like to think that our future depends on the very kind of human beings that Crossroaders are encouraged to be.